Granny always said,

"Hell's too good for Some People"

Dr. Larry Ivan Vass

iUniverse, Inc.
New York   Bloomington

Hell's Too Good For Some People

iUniverse books may be ordered through booksellers or by contacting:

iUniverse
1663 Liberty Drive
Bloomington, IN 47403
www.iuniverse.com
1-800-Authors (1-800-288-4677)

Because of the dynamic nature of the Internet, any Web addresses or links contained in this book may have changed since publication and may no longer be valid. The views expressed in this work are solely those of the author and do not necessarily reflect the views of the publisher, and the publisher hereby disclaims any responsibility for them.

ISBN: 978-1-4502-1663-0 (sc)
ISBN: 978-1-4502-1662-3 (ebook)

Printed in the United States of America

iUniverse rev. date: 5/7/2010

Table of Contents

Chapter One

A Time to Remember

The "times of our lives" can be times of struggle, or times of adventure, times of hardship, or times of blessings, times of unexpected calamity, and yet times of inexplicable excitement. There comes to all a time to ask the question, *"What are we that God should consider us?"* Yet a time to answer, *"We are wonderfully and fearfully made."* There is nothing more important to each of us than to discover that we live our lives according to a plan, a plan that will influence us to live in humble virtue, in boldness, selflessness, and servitude, or in darkness, fear, selfishness, and slavery. We may not have the answers or possess the understanding of our limitations and our dependence on that plan, but we are given repeated opportunities to seek for our purpose, our faith in the Planner, and for forgiveness when the answer comes.

So it was growing up in the hills of Virginia. Every day brought new experiences for those prepared to accept the challenges and meet them head on. Life was a struggle, doing the right thing exacting, and lessons learned plentiful.

I grew up atop the outrageously beautiful Blue Ridge Mountains. It was a mere eleven miles from where I lived to the federally maintained Blue Ridge Parkway that ran the crest of the majestic peaks from the Great Smokey Mountains in North Carolina to the Skyline Drive at Waynesboro, Virginia.

In the springtime the woodlands of the Blue Ridge would come to life with the purple and white blossoms of the mountain laurel and the rhododendron, the clusters of white bloom on the Bradford pear, the ivory colored bloom of the wild dogwood, the pale pink of the wild cherry, the lavender of the wisteria, and the brilliant red of the crabapple. The manicured grassy areas along the sides of the road and the fields beyond danced with the blooms of white daisies and Queen Anne's lace, yellow Blacked-Eyed Susans and dandelions, and the purple of creeping phlox and clover.

When autumn arrived, it tiptoed in on the heels of hot summer days and cool breezy nights. As if looking through the magnifying lens of a kaleidoscope, the leaves on the trees were launched into a blaze of colors that mirrored the oils spread about on an artist's pallet. The leaves on the deciduous trees changed from numerous hues of green to every color of the rainbow. The foliage on poplar trees exchanged their pale green for a brilliant yellow, maple trees for lemon yellow and nectarine orange, oak trees for fire-engine red and dirt brown, evergreens that never lost their needles retained their varying shades of green, and all the other trees turned to every color in between.

The dichotomy of life in the mountains mimicked the seasons: cruel one moment, blessed the next, sometimes a hardship, and other times a gift from God. As youth growing up as we did, many times life for my brother and me seemed outrageously overwhelming; but as we matured and were able to look back with some sense of objectivity, we realized that life here was truly glorious. Each and every thing that ever happened to us in our lives as children and as adults, we came to recognize as a culmination of life experiences that trained us, and as godly upbringing that inspired us and caused us to succeed in all that we ever tried.

Outsiders might ask, "How could you live like that?" Those of us on the inside could answer, "How could you not?" We might even add, "Why would one want to live any other way?" It's ironic how perspectives change! When young and living on the "inside," I would ask, "How can I possibly continue to live like this?" Now living on the "outside" and looking back with reflection, I answer, "Are you kidding me? How else <u>could </u>I have lived, and what better way was there?"

As bigger-than-life influences in our lives, my mother lived to the age of eighty-seven, and my father to ninety-one. Because of the magnetic pull of these mountains, Mom and Dad spent their entire lives here, never wishing to leave. In all those years, they actually left the mountains only twice. They once spent a week visiting relatives in Indiana and another week with their son, Lewis, when he lived on the coast of Virginia.

My parents are both gone now, but never will they be forgotten. It is their legacy that makes my stories timeless. These pages encompass an age that will never be forgotten, that stand still before us, live on in our very existence, and influence those that come after us.

Our years of growing up in these majestic mountains depicted a time that now seemed so hard, and yet, I could not imagine having grown up any other way. It was a time that one might want to forget, but it haunts you if you try. It floods your mind with heartaches and at the same time fills your soul with extreme gladness.

I have two siblings, a brother named Robert Lewis, who is three years older than me, and a sister with an American Indian name, Theoa, who is eleven years older than me.

There is indigenous Indian blood that courses through our veins. Our great-great grandmother is said to have been a full-blooded Cherokee Indian. In the only picture I have ever seen of her, she had a ruddy reddish complexion, and straight coarse black hair done up tightly in a bun on the top of her head. Out of the bun protruded an eagle's feather that pointed downward to the left. In the picture she is wearing a full length beaver coat and black leather boots that laced all the way to the knee.

You might consider my sister and me miracle children. I'll tell you about why I am later. After contracting epidemic paralytic poliomyelitis when she was twelve years of age, my sister has spent her entire life battling the pain and the crippling effects of the disease. Like a foreboding nightmare, this viral epidemic took its toll throughout the country during the middle to late 1940's, killing some, crippling others. It had spread like a brush fire driven by a Santa Anna wind. The doctors told my parents that their only daughter would never walk again. Of course they didn't know my sister very well! Thanks to the county doctor in our little "one-horse" hometown, Theoa did walk again. It was not a beautiful or a graceful walk, but a bipedal walk nevertheless. She went wherever she wanted to go, and still does.

Our family doctor had a swimming pool in his backyard, probably the only pool in the entire town and more than likely the only one in the whole county. He told my parents to bring Theoa to his house every day so that she could use his pool to do her physical therapy.

Day in and day out, my parents would take my sister to the doctor's house and help her into the water. Up to her neck in the water, Theoa would hold onto the side of the pool and attempt to move her legs. I am quite sure that trying to work out in that water every day without results must have seemed like an exercise in futility.

One glorious day, however, she did move one of her legs, not a lot, but she moved it. It wasn't long before she was able to move the other leg as well. Day after day, day in and day out, Theoa would get into the water, hold onto the side of the pool, and kick her legs. By the time she was fourteen years old, she had left her crutches behind and walked with only braces on her legs, legs that had severely atrophied as a result of the disease.

My sister's determination can only be described as absolutely ridiculous. The poliomyelitis had left her with one leg that was shorter than the other leg by three quarters of an inch. She walked with a limp and as she made each step, always with her weaker right foot leading, the toes would drag and the foot would end up being planted with a flop. When seated, Theoa was unable to raise her right foot without the aid of placing her hand under the bend of her knee to lift it. Yet in spite of this, she learned to drive Dad's Hudson automobile that was equipped with a straight-shift drive. Somehow, some way, she pushed in the clutch and applied the brake, all with her good left foot. She became a speed demon in spite of her semi-crippled condition.

When she was not yet old enough to legally drive, Theoa would back the Hudson the quarter of a mile down the single lane dirt and gravel drive to the highway to pick up the mail. When she did this she drove at top speed in reverse, not once wavering from a straight path or running off into the grass along the side of the drive. Coming to a screeching halt at the main highway, she would get out of the car and retrieve the contents of the mailbox. Getting back into the auto, Theoa would drive back to the house as fast as the car would go with the dust from the dirt road chasing after her. In that quarter mile she would move the gear shift through all three shift positions before sliding to a stop in front of the house.

During her rehabilitation a friend of the family by the name of Elmo, affectionately called "Mo," had started hanging around the house a great deal. He would come by after Theoa had returned home from her aquatic workouts bringing candy for her and chewing gum for me. When I spotted him coming into the house, I would run up to him and cry out, "Huh! Chew gum!" To this poor request for gum from a three year old, he would reach into his coat pocket and produce "Juicy Fruit." Of course, Mo got exactly what he wanted. I would take the gum and leave them alone for the time that he was visiting with my sister. Everyone was happy.

Theoa married Mo when she was only fifteen years of age. My parents not only allowed this to happen but I am quite sure they encouraged it. Undoubtedly, as parents, they would have been concerned about her marital prospects, especially given her medical condition.

Mo was nine years older than my sister, had a full-time job, and was a hard-working man. He always seemed to have treated my sister especially well for which I have always been grateful.

Not a very large man, Mo was only five feet six inches tall. He had some very peculiar characteristics and where he got them no one knows for sure. His father was a very stern, hard man. It was said that he could work a team of horses better than any man in that part of the country. Mo's mother was a quiet, humble woman who played the harpsichord, not only quite well, but with such elegance and flair that when you listened to her beautiful music, you were transported to distant places. Neither one of them exhibited the oddities Mo did.

When Mo was asked if he would like a refill of his coffee cup or if he would like another piece of pie or cake, his response was invariably, "Just a half-a-cup" or "Just a half-a-piece." Never, but never, did I ever see him take a full cup of anything or an entire piece of cake or pie in all the years that I have known him. Perhaps that explains why he always remained thin.

Another "different" thing about Mo was that he had to give something he was working on just one more turn, one more twist, or one more whack. Once after he had finished sharpening the blade on his lawnmower, in reattaching it to the shaft underneath, Mo had turned the nut that held the blade onto the shaft until, to everyone else's satisfaction, it was sufficiently tight. Of course he thought it needed "one more turn." That's when the wrench slipped off the nut and the newly sharpened blade took the tops off all the knuckles on my brother-in-law's right hand. Needless to say, that was a bloody mess. Mo was always covered in bandages and band aids.

Besides his many quirks, Mo was unbelievably hairy. It was as if he were a throwback to prehistoric man. In the summer months when it was time to mow and bail the hay, Mo came to help us haul in our hay and we in turn helped him. The hair on his neck, back, and arms was so thick and long that the hay seeds that fell from the straw and the dust that bellowed up from the mowed and raked fields clung tenaciously to his arms and back. When it came time to take a lunch break, we removed our shirts and went to the outdoor sink by the work shed to wash up. We would splash water over our entire upper bodies and lather up with Ivory soap. Mo's short stubby arms would resemble roots of trees covered in layer upon layer of snow white "Cool Whip." I was always mesmerized by the mounds of lather produced as he rubbed the bar of soap up and down his hairy arms. That long hair interacting with the sudsy action of the soap in the palm of his hand just kept producing and producing. That never ever happened to the hairless arms that I had. As a little kid, I was amazed.

Mo taught Lewis and me about a great many things when we were young. He even gave us a lesson on electric current. On separate occasions when he was using one of those early gasoline powered lawn mowers to mown the lawn for Dad before Lewis or I ever were old enough or big enough to do it ourselves, Mo introduced us to the flow of electricity. These mowers were hard to crank and did not have a retractable cord that one pulled to turn the two cycle engine over for starting. Mo asked Lewis once if he would like to help him crank the lawn mower. Lewis said, "Sure."

Mo said to him, "You hold the end of the spark plug while I pull the cord that I have wrapped around the starter shaft."

Lewis responded, "No way. When you pull the cord, I'll be shocked!"

Mo said, "Alright, I'll hold the spark plug and you pull the cord."

That seemed more like it, so Lewis agreed. Mo tested the pull cord around the spool on top the starter shaft to make sure it was attached firmly, handed the "T" handle of the pull cord to my brother, took hold of the spark plug, and said, "Okay, now pull the starter cord."

After he had taken hold of the spark plug, Mo placed his other hand near Lewis' ankle, and said, "Ready? Pull the cord."

Excited to be able to help, and smiling at the thought that now Mo would be the one to be shocked, Lewis pulled on the starter cord as hard as he could. At exactly the same time Mo grabbed Lewis' ankle. Instead of the engine firing, the electricity from the spark plug flowed from Mo's hand into Lewis' ankle. His hair stood on end and he started to gyrate about like a spinning top. When the electricity stopped flowing, Lewis fell to the ground as if he had been shot. Mo laughed at what he had done and said, "Let that be your first lesson in electricity."

He did a similar thing to me some years later. When I was about six or seven years old, it was a hot humid August day, and I was playing and running around the house in just my *Fruit of the Loom* underwear. Dad had to work at the hosiery mill that Saturday, so out of his respect for and love of my father, Mo mowed our yard. When I came around the corner of the house near the brick building where the lawn mower was kept, Mo was just finishing up and ready to shut down the lawnmower's engine.

The mower had no "on" and "off" switch, so in order to shut the engine off, a metal strip that was attached to the frame of the mower had to be pushed up against the spark plug. This would ground the engine and shut it off. To avoid receiving a shock one would push the metal strip up against the spark plug by using either a wooden stick, a pair of pliers with the handles covered in rubber, or a screw driver that had a plastic handle. As I came around the corner of the house chasing Susie, our black cocker spaniel, Mo grabbed me by the arm at the same time that he pushed the metal strip against the spark plug with an unprotected finger. The electricity coursed through him directly into me. I received an electric shock that caused me to dance about and made all my hair stand on end. What a lesson in electricity indeed! I also learned to be more aware of my much older fun-loving brother-in-law.

Before my parents' health started to fail, my brother-in-law had his own health issues. His kidneys had completely shut down from taking medicine for hypertension for over thirty years and after all that time the medicine had simply "blown out" his kidneys. Fortunately, Mo was able to retire before that happened. It was a good thing he had retired since he had to go to the hospital three days a week every week at five o'clock in the morning to be hooked up to a dialysis machine for four hours of blood cleansing. These treatments continued for years and years, right up to the time of his death.

I am the baby of the family. I have always been what you might call "unique" from the very beginning of my life. While pregnant with me, my mother developed *Bright's disease* in her third or fourth month of pregnancy. *Bright's disease* is an acute suppurative nephritis that has a short severe course, and results many times in death. She was advised by her doctor to abort me. The medical prognosis suggested that it would come down to either her life or mine. Mom thought and prayed about this long and hard and ultimately decided to risk it all. Her faith paid off. She lived and I'm telling you this story.

"Larry" was a popular name the year that I was born. I remember in my fifth grade homeroom, there were five "Larry's," no "Lawrence's", just Larry's. None of the other Larry's, however, had the middle name of "Ivan" like I did, even though it was supposed to be "Ian."

I was born at home and old Dr. Cox who delivered me was the one who gave me the name of Ivan. After my delivery and after Dr. Cox had washed up, he started filling out the paperwork for my birth certificate. Of course he knew what to place in the blank for the last name, so he asked, "First name?" and my mother responded, "Larry."

"Alright," the doctor grumbled (thinking that it should have been 'Lawrence'). "What have you chosen for his middle name?"

"My mother proudly replied, *"Ian."*

Dr. Cox, who was tall and gruff and robustly built, turned on my mother like an old grisly bear and growled at her, "What kind of g?!@! *d?!@!* name is that? Never heard of such!" he grumbled with yet another string of profanity. "If it has to begin with an 'I,' let's make it Ivan. At least we have all heard that g?!@! d?!@! name before." And so *Ivan* is the name he wrote down as my middle name on the birth certificate. In essence, my doctor determined my middle name, but that is of no consequence now.

I was a runt with a swollen belly like a poor third world country refugee until about the fourth or fifth grade. I was very picky about the foods that I ate. Nothing tasted good. No food enticed me to try it and nothing appealed to my immature culinary senses. The oxygen-starved veins under my skin gave the appearance of a pale bluish balloon that had been stretched tightly over a boney carcass with a white tuft of hair on top. Worried about how I was just not growing, developing, or advancing in cerebral things, my concerned parents took me to the doctor. I don't know what that mean old man gave me (yes! the same crotchety old man that had delivered me and given me my middle name), but I had to swallow this nasty-tasting green liquid every morning and every night for about a month. Personally, I wish I had never been given that foul-smelling, fecal-tasting medicine that only carrion eaters and ocean-bottom feeders could possibly have enjoyed. Since that time until now, I haven't stopped eating everything in sight. My palate has matured way too much! I've never met a bread, a cheese, or a meat I didn't like.

* * * * * *

Because I live in another state, a six and a half hour drive if traffic is light, I was unable to help my brother with Mom or Dad in their last days. For the final three to four months before Mom died, I would drive to my hometown every other Friday after work. Arriving around two o'clock in the morning, I would check into a hotel and spend the night. After spending most of Saturday with my parents, I had to return to my home in Maryland, because I had to preach on Sunday morning at an adult active community center called Southwinds. It made for a long, difficult, and too short a weekend, but that's what I had to do and wanted to do.

It was devastating to us all when Mom started losing her memory. After a couple of hours visiting with her and Dad, sometimes talking, sometimes just rocking in their big 'ole black-lacquered pine Boston Rocker, I would excuse myself and go down the hall to use their bathroom. I had to splash some cool water on my face to stay awake. Like so many elderly people, my parents kept the thermostat in their house set between seventy-six and seventy-eight degrees. It didn't take long in that heat to start nodding off. I did not drive all that distance to sit with them and sleep. Each time I returned to the den, Mom would see me coming down the hall and with a big grin spreading from ear to ear across her sweetly aged face, she would say to me in that wonderful Appalachian Mountain accent, "Well for heaven's sake, when did you get here?" I never laughed at my mom or the situation. It seemed appropriate at the time to simply say, "Just got here, Mom."

I would walk in behind her *Lazy Boy* where she was partially reclined, covered with a throw that she had crocheted herself many years ago, bend down and kiss her on the forehead, and say, "I love you, Mom. I just couldn't stay away any longer. I had to come to see you and Dad." That seemed to have pleased her to no end. It was as though she actually crooned a little as she wiggled about, lost in her big recliner.

When I was a child growing up in the hills of Virginia, my mom was a much larger woman than she was at the close of her life. She stood only five foot five, but at one time carried a large amount of weight in her thighs. Her weight reached one hundred ninety-five pounds when I was a teen-ager. At the end of her life she weighed less than eighty pounds. Getting old is definitely not for sissies or the faint of heart. Isn't it a shame that so many folks spend so much of their lives trying to lose weight, only to get sick and lose too much weight when it's needed the most to sustain their life. What an ironic twist of fate!

Looking at Mom's and Dad's wedding picture (when she was only fifteen and he eighteen), I often would think to myself, 'I wonder why in the world Dad ever married her anyway?' She really was somewhat homely with her large bucked front teeth. Of course when anyone got to know her, she was more beautiful to them than anyone they had ever known.

When I was in high school my mother had a dentist extract her upper front teeth. She had opted to have a partial denture made to straighten up her smile and literally put her teeth back inside her mouth behind her lips. As hard as that decision must have been, it seemed to have been the right one. The new and straight front teeth simply accentuated the wonderful smile that she had always had. It was a smile that could melt your heart.

Sometimes Mom would nod off to sleep while Dad and I discussed deep theological matters and talked about how good God had always been to our family. Dad would often get tears in his eyes when he talked about how blessed he had been all these years to have such a wonderful companion as "Mom" (as he had come to call her in their later years). Then he would say how wonderful it was to have three children such as Lewis and Theoa and me. He would always talk about what a wonderful sermon Lewis had preached last Sunday and would invariably remark, "That boy can do anything that he sets his mind to." And of course he believed Theoa could do anything that was set before her. Dad would often say, "She is simply a saint I tell you, a saint!" And to be honest, I could find no fault with his assessment. Often after a few refreshing minutes of sleep, Mom would wake up, see me sitting there with Dad, and in wonderment almost like a child, she would ask, "Well, when did you get here?" It was not unusual to experience as many as six "visits" with her in a single afternoon.

Dad was a wonderful neighbor, a generous man, a well liked and highly regarded man. He could also be a hard man. I didn't actually realize how loving and caring he was to my brother and me until we were both grown and had been gone from home for many years.

Lewis and I had harbored resentment in our hearts for having "missed" our childhood. However, the most extraordinary thing, at least for me, happened some thirty-five years after I had left home. My wife and I were visiting my parents one weekend when out of the blue Dad said, "You know Larry I must apologize to you."

Unsure of where he was coming from and where he was heading with this, I slowly drew out the question, "Okay….for what do you need to apologize?" The words he said literally shocked me!

"You know Larry," he began, "I never realized that I was depriving you and your brother from being able to enjoy your childhoods. I was just so proud of you two that I never considered that having you boys work like men was wrong. I never meant you two any harm. I was just so proud of you. I am sorry that I made you boys work so hard. I… I am sorry that I never let you experience what children should experience."

By the time he had finished his speech, I was an emotional wreck, shaking all over and crying uncontrollably. I got up out of my chair and walked over to him. Bending down, I put my arms around his shoulders and my head on his neck. I kissed him on the cheek and said, "Thank you, Dad. You have no idea how much what you have just said means to me. There is nothing else to say and nothing else to do. All is forgiven. Thank you, Dad, for making things right!"

What a cleansing! What a healing! My father was a much bigger man than I had ever given him credit for. In fact he was a much bigger man than I would ever be. I felt ashamed for having harbored those ill feelings toward him for all those years. I had suppressed my love and held onto all that negativity toward a man who truly loved me and nurtured me as best as he could. He was a man who survived the hardship of living in the mountains during the Great Depression, knowing nothing but hard times. Like so many others, he had to work diligently to pull himself up by the boot straps just to survive. He had to be tough and thought that if Lewis and I were ever going to make it in this world we would have to be taught to be tough as well. I'm just thankful that he never named me "Sue."

I know that Dad had a similar conversation with my brother some time after he had talked to me. Lewis and Dad were walking across the hill above my father's house looking at all the beautiful things that God had created. Before Dad had actually offered any apology, Lewis said to him, "You know, Dad, you are probably the most level headed man that I have ever known."

Taking this as a compliment, Dad responded, "Why, thank you son. Why do you think so?"

Lewis turned and looked him square in the eyes and without cracking a smile, said matter-of-factly, "Because the chewing tobacco that you chew always leaves a stain at the corners of your mouth evenly."

They walked on for a little while in silence. Dad finally saw the humor in Lewis' statement and laughed out loud. He had quit smoking unfiltered Camel cigarettes after a fifty-year habit which started when he was only twelve years old. Once he had put down the smokes, however, he had begun to chew tobacco to "fill the void." Everyone had tried to persuade him not to indulge in the nasty habit of chewing and spitting.

"I get your point, son," he said. He then proceeded to make his apology to my brother in the same manner as he had to me. Regardless of what the world today thinks, it takes a big man to humble himself, especially to his grown sons. We are forever grateful for the tremendous lessons he taught us, and this is certainly one of them.

Chapter Two

A Battle of Canes and Death Comes

"She's dead!"

I pulled the phone away from my ear and stared at it for a few seconds as if the phone itself had spoken to me. I slowly put it back to my ear and mouthed the words, "What did you say?"

Again those same words, "She's dead! Your mother passed away this afternoon."

I had been home only a couple of days from one of my visits with her. My wife's voice came across that receiver like some hollow ethereal echo. The words, "She's dead! Your mother passed away this afternoon," entered my ear and rattled around like a handful of marbles in a metal bucket. I stopped breathing! I couldn't cry! I couldn't speak! I couldn't even mourn!

In February Mom had lost her balance going into her bathroom and had fallen across the bathtub. The femur just below the ball-joint of her right hip snapped in two and jutted out through the skin. When my brother called me about that accident, I just knew that there was trouble ahead. Everyone "knows" that when elderly people fall and break their hips, they often die of pneumonia without ever recovering from the fall. But Mom was different. An orthopedist performed surgery on her fractured femur. A metal rod was shoved down the shaft of the largest long bone in the body, a few titanium screws were placed to hold things together, and my mother started physical therapy. Unbelievably, she fully recovered. She had to walk with a cane, but the fact remained, Mom was up and walking. It just might be that spunkiness is a genetic trait that is shared between mother and daughter.

Something however, seemed to have happened to Mom as a result of that fall. You might say it "rattled her brain." From that time forward, the little spells of forgetfulness, those periods of not recognizing people that she had not seen for some time, the occasions of not wanting to eat or even realizing that she was hungry (in spite of the rumblings coming from her stomach), the occasional outburst of foul language and meanness, everything accelerated. By the time Mom turned eighty-seven on August third, she had deteriorated so rapidly that she had become bed-ridden, was not able to recognize anyone, had terrible bed sores on her back and buttocks, could not take in any food, and was totally incontinent and incoherent. She had lost down to a mere seventy-nine pounds, skin stretched tightly over her small skeletal frame.

A few days before my last visit, Mom had been lying on the hospital bed in her room at home staring into space. One of the caregivers who was present at her bedside witnessed her pointing her right finger toward the ceiling in the corner of the room and overheard her say plainly, "Look at all the beautiful people." A few days later on the very day she died, I was told that Mom had been uttering unintelligible gibberish. Just minutes before she passed, however, she was heard to have exclaimed quite clearly, "Praise the Lord; He's my Savior."

Hearing those words made it hard for me to be sad or remorseful. My mom had lived a long full life with a man with whom she had been in love with from the age of fourteen, and with whom she had shared her life for almost seventy-two years. She was in pain; she was unable to eat, to communicate, or able to recognize people around her. She needed to be with Jesus. She had run her race, she had finished the course, and she was ready to receive her crown.

One of her crowns was so obvious, manifested as long lines of family and friends that had come to her viewing to show their respect. The procession of hundreds of people went on for hours. After each person had stopped to gaze upon my sweet mother's face, and had spoken his or her condolences to my dad, my brother, my sister, and me, they retreated to the sanctuary of the Vaughn-Guynn Funeral Home Chapel and seated themselves. The place was filled and still more people came, not only to pay their respects to a wonderful godly woman whom they had known their entire lives, but they had come in droves to see our family. Dad and Mom had been like parents and grandparents to the folks in this small southern town. Everyone either knew them or knew about them, and those who knew them personally, loved them. They realized that they would not only miss my mom, who seemed like their own mother, but my dad soon as well.

People remained until the funeral home director went to each one individually and announced that the funeral home was about to close. They needed to go home.

Because I had left home at the age of seventeen to go to college and dental school (and much later seminary), and lived most of my adult life in Maryland, these people never really knew me. In the receiving line I talked with first cousins for the first time in maybe forty years or more. They didn't know me and I certainly didn't know them. Many of us had to be introduced to one another, and when I think back about that now, it makes me sad.

Mom wore a pendant around her neck, which my wife Charlotte and I had given to her for Christmas a few years earlier. It was a sterling silver angel with a child of gold being held in and surrounded by the angel's wings. The Funeral Director asked me if I wanted it back after the funeral and I said, "No." Mom had loved that pendant and I wanted it with her. I obviously wasn't thinking clearly or far enough ahead. Mother is with Jesus now and her deteriorated, cancer-eaten body is all that there is in the ground. I wish I had said, "Yes," that I wanted that pendant back. I could have given it to my firstborn granddaughter, Loralei, so that whenever she wore it, I could imagine my mother's smiling face.

Mom's funeral was the next morning. Two of her favorite preachers, unrelated but with the same last name of Bowman, performed the service and my brother Lewis talked about Mom and the family in a sort of eulogy. I was invited to say whatever was on my heart.

I had not really prepared anything specific on which to speak, but during the long drive from Maryland to my hometown in Virginia (while my wife called everyone she could think of on her cell phone to let them know that Mom had died and what the funeral arrangements were) the story of Mephibosheth in the book of Second Samuel of the Old Testament laid heavy on my mind.

The story told about (King) David coming into the court of King Saul after having killed the giant Goliath. David and Saul's son,

Jonathan, became close bosom buddies. Years later, King Saul and his son Jonathan were killed by David's men in a battle for the kingdom. David was heartbroken over the death of his best friend, Jonathan. He issued an edict to determine if there were any left from the house of Saul that he might show them kindness for Jonathan's sake. There was indeed a servant by the name of Ziba whom David commanded to be brought before him. When Ziba came into the presence of the king, David asked him if there were any of the family of Saul that might be left to whom he could show them the kindness of God. Ziba told David that Jonathan had had a son. He was lame and was living in the house of Machir, the son of Amiel, in Lo-debar. Upon hearing this King David sent some of his soldiers to fetch this lame boy from Machir's house. When Jonathan's son, Mephibosheth, was brought before King David, he was fearful and shook like a leaf on a tree on a windy day. He fell prostrate upon the floor as if dead for he knew that when a man took the throne and became king, he usually had everyone in the family of the previous king put to death. So here was Mephibosheth, shaking in his sandals before the king who said to him, "Fear not Mephibosheth, for I will surely show you kindness for Jonathan your father's sake, and you shall eat bread at my table continually....you shall eat at my table as one of the king's sons."

Then I contrasted the story of Mephibosheth with my mother. Mephibosheth stood before King David with fear and trepidation and was told that henceforth he would dine at the King's table as one of his sons. My mother stood <u>without</u> fear and in full confidence before King Jesus. She knew that she was there to receive her reward, the reward promised to her before the foundation of the world that henceforth, she would dine at the King's table as one of His daughters and share in the Kingdom as a joint heir.

Mom was interred in her family's cemetery overlooking the farm on which I was raised and from which my brother and I had hauled hundreds of trailer loads of rocks. Not only was it a sad day to say goodbye to our mother and to hold up our father who was so frail, but it was also sad to see the farm that my brother and I had slaved on for all those childhood years now stand in ruin. Thistles grew profusely where corn once stood tall. Scrub black pines wobbled in the breeze where oats once waved. Fence rows bore a heavy burden of briars, poison ivy, and kudzu where once they ran clean and unencumbered. Mom was gone. The once manicured farm that I had grown up on was gone. My father would soon die of loneliness from the loss of his best friend and wife of seventy-two years. Without a doubt, childhood memories would someday be all that was left.

Maybe memories would be enough. Perhaps we put too much emphasis on keeping people alive longer than they were meant to be. It is never a pleasant thing to lose loved ones, especially those who brought you into this world and loved you through your journey.

I am not suggesting that as soon as someone starts to fail in their health, or in their recognition of people around them, or in their ability to take care of themselves that they should be discarded like a pair of old shoes, no longer pretty, comfortable, or functional. I am suggesting that when these things start to manifest themselves that we don't try to second guess with "what ifs," or try to hold onto the shell that loved one used to fill, or to the "life at any cost" as if that produces the memories we so desperately cling to. Until their dying breath, morally we should do everything possible to maintain these loved ones' dignity, to make them as comfortable as possible, to love them with the love of Christ, and provide for their every need. When the time does come to let them go, we must release them with their dignity intact. We can then take some solace and even pride in knowing that we did everything humanly possible to love them, maintain them, and care for them as offspring should.

Lovingly release the memories that remind you how desperately these loved ones struggled at the end of their days, how much pain they must have been in, how different the reality of who they were at death from what we remember them to have "always" been. Memories should be reserved for loving them as they were when they loved us, and sacrificed for our comfort, our education, and our well-being. Memories are naturally filtered to eliminate those things that are painful to recall, and to eliminate all "the garbage" that has cluttered up our lives.

I refuse to dwell on the fact that Mom didn't recognize me when I came to visit her in her last days, nor on how she lost weight down to below eighty pounds, how she refused to eat even though her stomach would growl, and even said mean and nasty things to my father when he tried so desperately to get her to eat. Alzheimer's is a horrible disease that robs its victims of their memory, but not their loved ones' precious recollections.

When my mother died, I chose to remember her as she was, not as she had become at the end of her life. I intend to always remember her as the woman with the sweet countenance, not as the woman with the grimace of pain on her face. She was loving and kind, not mean and grouchy, giving and gracious, not hoarding and acrimonious, spiritual and God-fearing, not secular and self-righteous. The attributes that my mother possessed before Alzheimer's took her away are the attributes that will forever fill my mind, the ones on which I will intentionally dwell.

About a month after Mom had died of complications from her Alzheimer's on August 16th (the day before my wedding anniversary and two days before my birthday), Dad decided that it didn't look right for one of the three young women that we had hired as caregivers (for both him and Mom) to stay overnight in his house. It was somewhat amusing considering Dad was ninety years old and the women were thirty-five to fifty years younger than he. However, one had to respect his feelings and his moral compass. He had come to the conclusion that he needed to move into an assisted-living facility for at least a month on a "trial basis." It also seemed like a good idea to his three children, who loved him and wanted only the best for him.

After a month, Dad already knew in his heart that he was never going "home" again. He gave instructions to sell the now empty house he and Mom had shared for decades. He had come to the conclusion that it was best to remain in the assisted-living complex and wait to go to his *real* home when he would be reunited with my sweet mother, and united to our precious Lord and Savior, Jesus the Christ.

It was heart wrenching to witness Dad's decline from September until he died the following April from complications of pneumonia. I believe, however, Dad simply didn't want to live anymore without his bide of almost seventy-two years. I can only imagine the sweet reunion they shared when he left this earth to join her in heaven.

I was so thankful that I had continued to travel to Virginia to visit with Dad just as I had gone to see Mom before she had passed away. God blessed me with that "extra" time with my father.

Living in an assisted-living facility had its moments. My brother called me often, keeping me apprised of the details of what was going on with our father. Somehow Dad had gotten it into his head that the woman living in the room next to his was running a brothel. On one occasion he informed my brother that the lady owned all the "apartments" from his room all the way to the end of the building, and that she was a madam of at least ten girls. Regardless of how many times Lewis told Dad that the lady next door was not running a whore house, his words fell on deaf ears.

One Saturday afternoon the peace and quiet on Dad's hall was disrupted abruptly by the sound of *clack, clack, clack, clack*, interspersed with shouting and screaming. Attendants from the front office ran down the hall and found Dad, dressed in his beige all-weather Members Only jacket, his plaid English snap-bill cap, and his woolen plaid high-top house slippers, having it out with the woman who occupied the room across the hall. They were dueling with their canes in earnest, clearly with the intent of doing each other bodily harm. No one knew why they disliked each other so much. They apparently had never known one another before becoming residents at the assisted-living facility.

With their arms locked around my father's waist, staff members dragged him from the room of his nemesis. They screamed murderous words at each other and waved their canes in the air in threatening jesters. The next day the lady was moved to another wing of the facility to keep them separated, and the feud quietly and finally came to an end.

Of all the strange things that my father ever said to my brother and me, the strangest was that every night Mom came to his bed and would sleep with him. The next morning, however, she would have slipped out of bed and be gone by the time he awakened. Lewis and I told him repeatedly that was not possible since Mom had gone to be with the Lord. He still insisted that she had been there the night before and would implore us to just help him look for her. We never really had to look for Mom, for in a few minutes Dad would have forgotten that he had wanted to search for her at all.

I have often pondered over what Dad said after Mom's death, and I think that perhaps Mom *was* there at nights with him, not in body, but in spirit. Over seventy-three years of knowing someone and knowing them intimately for almost seventy-two years of that time certainly can cause one's mind to see things as they once were. Memories are sweet and they keep us going during the tough times.

In the relatively short (compared to Mom and Dad) number of years that Charlotte and I have been married there have been many times when we finish one another's sentences. You come to the place where you know one another so well that many times words are unnecessary. A touch can substitute for words, and a look can speak volumes. One can bring up some subject and the other will say, "I was just thinking that very thing." When your very soul can *feel* what your spouse feels, your mind can track what their thoughts are, your heart aches when you know your "other half" is not happy but sad, it is then that you know you are in absolute harmony with one another and God is an integral part of your marriage.

Certainly that's how it was with Mom and Dad. The Bible says, when a couple marries, they become as one. As one, Dad could feel Mom's presence and I have no doubts he could *see* and *feel* her right there beside him. The attendants kept Dad busy during the day, but perhaps at night when he was the loneliest, that's when he missed her the most and felt her presence.

I am convinced Dad's death was the result of having lost his companion of seventy-two years. He just didn't want to live without her a day longer. Anyone can understand that, even if they haven't experienced such a close personal loss in their own lives. I have been married to my wife a mere eighteen years, yet the thought of having to live without her smiling face to greet me in the mornings, to live without her little annoyances that I have come to cherish more than anything in this world, to not be able to hold her hand when we walk on the beach or meander through a mall, not to be able to talk with her everyday, even if its only on the phone, not to be able to say, "I love you" every night when we turn out the lights, is possibly more than I could or even would want to bear. I can't even pretend to fathom how my father must have felt when his companion of over seven decades died leaving him alone in a world he had shared with her all his adult life. I can only imagine how he must have felt when his "right arm" had been ripped away, when his better half had vanished, when his next breath would not come without extreme effort, or when he finally didn't care if it did or not. When death creeps up from the dark abyss, it disrupts and depletes families. It shakes the very foundations of life. At one time or another everyone has to come to grips with its reality and grapple with the issue of personal mortality.

Chapter Three

Snowstorms, Sleet, and Drunken Cows

Working on a dairy farm was a demanding life, seven days a week, every week, month, and year. It required herding up the cattle before daybreak, milking them and feeding them before going off to school in the mornings, and then milking and feeding them upon returning home from school every afternoon. Of course we were never "off" on weekends. My brother and I worked all summer long plowing and planting, spraying and fertilizing, mowing and putting up the hay, building and mending fences, and removing those tons upon tons of "cursed" rocks from the fields. We hauled enough rocks off the land to have literally been able to build a four foot high rock fence around the entire perimeter of our hundred acre farm. Besides working on our own farm, my brother and I would hire ourselves out to plow and sow alfalfa, mow and rake hay, and pick up and haul the hay into barns for other people.

One humid, blisteringly hot summer day, my brother was mowing a field for a farmer on River Hill, an area of the county about as far away from home as we would ever have ventured to mow or plant seed for anyone. River Hill was that part of the county that bordered on Big Reed Island Creek. Many times the land there would be forty-five degrees from vertical. In other words, the angle of the land was steep. Most of the time people would have to work these fields with teams of horses, but my brother and I at ages nine and twelve thought that we were invincible and able to do anything. We would mow and rake grass and plant alfalfa with our tractor on land that most people would never have attempted to work. Dad allowed us to do this work of course. It could have been out of ignorance, not being cognizant of how steep the land was or how dangerous the job might have been, but the majority of the time it was because he wanted to showcase us as the two most terrific, industrious boys in all of Carroll County, Virginia. In a kind of warped sense of pride, Dad loved to have "his little men" do work that no sane grown person would have attempted.

On this particularly memorable day, Lewis was mowing one of those extremely steep fields while our mother's adult brother, Rex, was mowing nearby in another field (a field that was not nearly as steep and could be worked over with a tractor quite easily).

Lewis was certainly a mighty mite at age twelve, but he was also "vertically challenged." Many times he remained standing when working with the tractor in order to reach the brake pedals and the clutch. The field in which he was mowing that day required going straight up and down the hill to prevent the tractor from possibly flipping over. When he had mowed about half way down the hill the right rear tire of the tractor dropped into a hole that was completely hidden by the grass. The unsuspected jolt propelled my brother over the hood of the Ford tractor onto the ground in front of the oncoming rear-mounted sickle. With his wind knocked out, Lewis laid on the ground struggling to catch his breath. The blade of the sickle that was slivering back and forth came skimming along the surface of the ground a mere foot or two from the top of his head. He was unable to move a muscle, partly from the weakness of not being able to get any oxygen into his deflated lungs, and partly out of shear fright. Just when the oscillating mowing blade was about to bury its sharp prongs into the top of my brother's head, the right rear tire of the tractor dropped into another hidden hole. The rear-mounted mowing machine blade smacked hard against the ground and then bounced high into the air. It came down just beyond my brother's feet. By the grace of God, it missed him entirely.

Without its driver the tractor continued on in low gear down the hill. My brother was finally able to sit up after the blade bounced over him. He watched the tractor until it came to a stop against a large black oak tree at the river's edge. Within minutes the engine stalled out. Not once did Lewis think about trying to catch the run-away tractor. His entire body shook from fright and he was chilled to his very core in spite of the summer heat. As God had done time and time again, He saved my brother from death or possible mutilation. The God we serve is indeed a great and mighty God.

There was always something that made the miraculous seem ironic. When my brother was tossed from the tractor, he landed in a groundcover of poison oak, a plant to which my brother is highly allergic. By the time Lewis got home that night, his face was scarlet, his arms were blood red from scratching and his eyes were swollen shut. Perhaps God does have a sense of humor or maybe He was trying to tell our father something. Could it be my brother shouldn't have been out there at that early age doing that kind of work? Only God knew.

* * * * * *

When that summer and fall finally ended, the cold weather was upon us. For the next several years the winters seemed to grow longer and the snow and ice storms more severe. The cold was colder and the snow was deeper and fell more often.

A winter snow and ice storm that is still on the record books for the longest stretch of cold winter weather and the deepest snows happened three years after the near fatal accident my brother faced when he was thrown from the tractor. By Thanksgiving we had already experienced several snowstorms and had missed three or four days of school.

This was the winter of nineteen hundred fifty-seven/fifty-eight, the year we had to attend classes six days-a-week until mid-July to make up for all the time lost from school due to all the snow and ice. This was one of the most unforgettable times of my life. I was twelve years old and after it had snowed thirty-seven inches, part of the snow was blown by the wind into ten to twelve foot deep drifts. That was promptly topped off with sleet. One could walk across the snow without even breaking through it.

When we heard that heavy snows were coming, we thought we would outwit Mother Nature by parking the car at the end of our long driveway at the state highway. However, with sustained high winds for days, monumental snowdrifts buried the highways. No one was going anywhere.

That night it snowed another thirty plus inches; the wind blew **that** snow into even higher drifts; and more sleet came down on top of that. By the time it had stopped snowing and sleeting and the wind had stopped blowing, we had more than five feet of snow on the ground and ten to fifteen foot drifts across not only our driveway but across the state highways as well.

That great winter storm affected almost every aspect of people's lives. Some of our cows were trapped in the deep snow in the woods at the backside of our farm. They could not or would not come to the barn for shelter. The weight of the cows caused them to break through the ice and snow and since the snow was so deep and crusted over with ice, their hooves didn't even touch the ground. They would have remained suspended by the ice and snow and would have frozen to death if we had not made a way for them to come in.

One cow in particular, one of our best milk cows we called Bessie, had gotten stranded on the back side of the hill behind the cinder block barn. Bessie had already given up and without me making a way for her and beating on her and yelling at her she would have stayed where she was until she completely froze to death. Without constant prodding she would not have budged. I worked feverishly with a shovel to break up the ice and snow in front of the unmoving bovine, and then I would smack her on the hip with the back flat side of the shovel to make her move forward into the clearing I had just created. I remember crying all the while that I was trying to get her to the barn. It was not only very hard work, but I was tired, frustrated, and cold myself.

I was so cold that my tears froze as they ran down my cheeks. I was so cold my fingers grew numb. I was so cold that my wind-blown hair sticking out from underneath my toboggan was frozen solid. I was so cold that my pant legs were frozen as stiff as stove pipes. In fact, my pants were so frozen that when I finally went into the house and took them off, I was able to stand them up in the corner until they thawed out.

The wind coming across the hill above the barn was blowing so fiercely that I could feel my body being pushed along as if I were being shoved by an invisible hand. When the blowing snow struck the exposed parts of my face, it burned as if the snow hitting my skin were desert sand.

At the point when both the cow and I were just about to give up, I heard a loud racket that sounded like exploding dynamite. I stopped in my tracks and looked around. There was no sign of smoke or flying debris. I resumed breaking the snow in front of the beleaguered cow. The sound of an explosion occurred a second time. Once again I stood completely still and surveyed my surroundings. I looked into the brilliant blue sky for a jet that might have broken the sound barrier, not an uncommon occurrence where we lived; but there was no jet.

"*Caboom!*" I just happened to be looking toward the snow buried state highway that was approximately a half mile from where I stood. A ball of fire the size of a basketball ran along an electric power line from the pole at the top of the hill nearest our driveway to the next pole at the foot of the hill. A twisted multi-wire electric cable had been blown loose from the ceramic attachment on the first pole. Whenever a hard gust of wind topped the crest of the hill and rushed headlong down its slope, the loose power line would be blown against one of the other power lines that were still attached. Every time this happened, an explosion would occur and a ball of fire would travel the length of the line from that pole to the next. When the ball of fire hit the second pole it would explode into a million firefly-like cinders that produced a second sound just as loud as the first.

Watching the creation of the balls of fire and then seeing them explode scared me half to death. At age twelve I did not understand that if the loose power line snapped in two and fell to the ground the electricity running through the snow would peter out long before it reached me or the exhausted cow. I was under the impression that if the power line came crashing to the ground the cow and I would be fricasseed by the electricity traveling through the snow.

My adrenaline started pumping at an unbelievable rate. As if on performance enhancing drugs I started breaking off huge chunks of frozen snow and tossing them over my left shoulder. I must have looked like a snow blower in Minnesota in mid-winter. I would whack the cow on the hip with the shovel and she would move forward into the clearing. Over and over I broke off a chunk of ice and snow, throw it over my shoulder, and smack the cow on the hip. Finally we reached the auxiliary barn and I was able to force open the door blocked by drifted snow, and push the old cow into one of its three stalls. The exhausted cow stumbled forward and fell onto the floor that had been covered with fresh straw the day before. I came in right behind and dropped to my knees beside her. I pitched forward and laid my head on the cow's side. There we lay gasping for air.

After finishing his chores, my brother had gone to the house to warm himself. He and Mom had been watching me work feverishly to get the cow into the barn, but had stopped watching after the cow and I had disappeared into the gray clap-boarded building. Perceiving that we were finally safe, they breathed a sigh of relief.

After more than an hour, however, there was no Larry. I had never come to the house and Mom had started to worry. She asked my brother if he had seen me after the cow and I had entered the barn, and of course he hadn't. In spite of respecting what Mark Twain had once written, *"The worst tragedies of my life never even happened,"* Mom asked Lewis to go to the barn and make sure that both the cow and her son were indeed alright. After all, a twelve year old boy who appeared physically fit and had grown up working hard on a dairy farm could still drop dead with a heart attack from all that exertion!

Lewis' clothes were wet through and through from thawing out on the grate that covered the oil furnace between the dining area and the den. He had to put on a whole new set of outer wear to go back out into the cold to see what had happened to his little brother.

With a grumpy attitude, Lewis burst through the screen door on the back porch and headed for the grey-slatted building off to the right of the main cinderblock barn. It was a mere hundred yards of walking, but he was exhausted by the time he reached the three-stall barn. After plodding his way though three feet of snow, he managed to reach the front of the shed. He made his way around to the other side where he had seen me enter with the cow about ninety minutes earlier. The wind had blown more snow up against the door to the stall so Lewis had to put forth some serious effort to pull the door open against the banked white powder. There we were! The exhausted cow was lying on her side on the fresh straw fast asleep. With my head resting on her flank, I lay on my back asleep as well. In my brother's way of thinking, half his life had been spent being aggravated at me for not holding up my end of the work to his expectation, yet he admitted later he didn't have the heart to disturb this surreal scene - beast and boy asleep on the hay. To my way of thinking, I'm surprised he didn't kick me while I lay there.

When we were children my older brother and I went at each other all the time. In spite of the way it appeared, we loved each other and would always defend each other against all outsiders.

The next day after all the inclement weather had finally ceased, the sky was bluer and clearer than I can ever remember it being before. It seemed as though you could see forever. Mom went into the backyard and gathered a dishpan full of pure white snow and made snow ice cream. Oh! What memories! We ate that homemade ice cream and drank hot Dr Pepper with lemons and cinnamon sticks. Those were some good times.

The snowfall was so enormous in that record breaking winter storm that it completely covered my brother's '58 Chevy pickup. The only part of his truck that could be seen was the side mirror sticking out on the driver's side. Lewis and I didn't even attempt to shovel it out for a couple of weeks. What would have been the point? The quarter mile drive from the main highway to our house was covered by four to six foot drifts of snow. The white powder was so deep that we were unable to use our farm tractor with its rear mounted snow blade to clear out the driveway.

Over the next few days Lewis and I played for hours on end on top of the ice-covered snow on the steep hill in front of our house. The run was close to a half mile from the top of the hill in front of our house down to the springhead. Because of the ice that had fallen on top of the snow we didn't even need a sled. After taking just a couple of steps, we would belly flop onto the crystalline ice-covered ground and fly down that hill like a rocket. We had already plowed that hill to sow some winter wheat, but the weather never afforded us the opportunity. The snow and the ice had softened the plow furrows somewhat. As we went sliding down the hill on our stomachs we would laugh the whole way. We were being tickled the entire trip.

Like so many things we did growing up on the farm, this too was a little risky. Unlike riding a sled with steel runners, if we wanted to turn to the right, we dug into the ice covered snow with the toe of our right boot or our left if we wanted to go left. We wore bulky combat brogans so that when we pushed down hard with the toe, the thick leather soles that stuck out about a half inch beyond the shoe would dig into the ice and we could turn. Because the ice covered snow was so hard, however, it took "forever" to negotiate a turn. After we had a few run-ins with the rock that was piled high around the springhead at the bottom of the hill, we learned quickly that we needed to start our turns sooner than later.

We continued sliding down that hill on our stomachs and crawling on all fours back to the top. We did this the whole day long until it was almost dark. Since we had turned all the cows dry from milking and some of them were nursing their calves anyway, we didn't have to milk the cows, just feed them. When the sun started going down

Mom came out onto the front porch of our house and called us to come in for diner.

I thought my ears had been covered all day, but I was wrong. They had actually come out from underneath my toboggan by noon. After I had gone inside for diner, I had to pick out the ice that had caked into the folds of my ears. For awhile I thought my ears were frozen to the point they were going to fall off. They stung so badly that they felt like they were on fire. I'm surprised Lewis and I didn't get frost bite and lose our ears. Not only our ears but our toes burned and ached for hours.

We sat as closely as humanly possible to the grate in the floor between the dining room and the den. The grate covered a central oil furnace that was in the basement. All the heat came up through the rectangular shaped grate and warmed only the immediate area well, with a little heat spreading out sparingly to the rest of the house. Once you moved three or four feet away from the register you could feel the difference.

At bedtime we took the flannel blankets off our beds and laid them over the grate until they were so hot they felt like they were about to burst into flames. Lewis and I would race like banshees into our bedroom and hop into our bunk beds. Mom would come running into our room with the hot blankets and throw them over us. After tucking them in around our entire bodies, she would throw a homemade quilt or two over us, and then a chenille bedspread on top of that. With only our noses sticking out, we were set for the night. Wrapped up like a worm in a cocoon, we remained warm all night long. Folks who have only experienced central heat and air conditioning have no idea the adventures they have missed.

After being snowed in for a couple of weeks and after attempting to shovel our way out, Dad came to the realization that his two "wonder boys" had only removed the snow drifts from the driveway one third the way from the house to the highway. He finally had to call on a man he knew who owned a bulldozer to come and clear the snow off the drive. Since there was fencing on both sides of the driveway, the bulldozer could only push the snow straight ahead. With nowhere else to go, the operator piled all the frozen white powder in the front yard of the house. When he had finished piling the snow up, it was as high as the gable of the house. That snow remained there until it finally melted sometime in late July. The driveway wasn't paved in those days; at the bottom of the pile of snow was gravel and dirt picked up by the dozer blade as it pushed the snow ahead of it. The grass died in the front yard where the snow, gravel, and dirt had laid so long. To restore the area, we had to disk under the dead grass and reseed the whole area. What a chore that was!

After a chilly spring, summer came in as if someone had left open the door to a blast furnace. Maybe that was God's way of dealing with our complaints of how severe the winter had been. Human nature is like that; you complain when it's too cold and you complain when it's too hot. Regardless, farm life returned to normal, hard work and all.

Whether in the cold of winter or in the heat of summer there was always an adventure associated with one or more of our cattle. We had on our farm a cow we had named 'Ole Mousie. She was given that name because she was colored like a cartoon mouse we used to see on TV, and she moved at the same pace as that Mexican mouse did when he was drunk. Whenever the cattle didn't come to the barn on their own at milking time, Lewis or I would have to go round them up and drive them in. All the other cows usually came to the barn when they were called, but 'Ole Mousie just poked along, slowly bringing up the rear.

Many times Lewis would already be at the front of the barn directing the cows into their stalls to start the milking process when he would see me coming across the hill toward the gap. I would be riding on the back of 'Ole Mousie. Sometimes I would have both my feet on the hocks of the cow's hind legs, holding on to her tail, just singing away as she walked slowly to the barn. Most cows would have bucked other people off, but not me. I rode on their backs, set off cherry bombs on their heads, hung underneath them as they walked, but they paid me no mind.

My brother was married when he was only sixteen to his seventeen year old bride, Betty. They lived with Mom and Dad (and of course me) until they both graduated from high school and left home to work. Betty had seen many of the antics I had done with the cows that probably no one else would ever have tried, except maybe a rodeo hand. She would be the first to say, "All this is true. Lewis and Larry do not make this stuff up."

On one occasion 'Ole Mousie had gotten into some wild cherry leaves on trees that had been cut down on the farm next to ours. Several limbs of the felled trees hung over the fence between the farms. The leaves were evidently very tasty to 'Ole Mousie. By the time the inquisitive bovine started munching on the leaves they had begun to wilt, and by whatever biological process, had become intoxicating to a cow. All the other cattle had gone straight to the barnyard to be fed and submit to being milked, but 'Ole Mousie didn't show. My brother had driven four of the cows into the designated area, had washed the dried dirt and feces off their utters with hot sudsy water, and placed suction tubes of the milking machines onto their teats. I went to the back of our farm to find the missing Guernsey. By the time I found 'Ole Mousie and had driven her to the gap to the barn lot, Lewis had finished milking all the other cows.

It had taken me over an hour to both locate 'Ole Mousie and drive her home to within sight of the milk barn. She wobbled and weaved and staggered as she walked. The cow was as inebriated as a drunken sailor and every time she took a step, she stopped. I had to constantly smack her on the hip with the palm of my hand and yell at her to encourage her to take the next step.

Lewis had come out of the barn on numerous occasions to see if I had found 'Ole Mousie and had brought her in. Once he saw me coming with that 'ole cow, he went back into the barn. After a few minutes, however, he heard a blood curdling scream coming from the area of the gap where he had seen me with 'Ole Mousie. My brother came running out of the barn and looked to the gap where he had last seen me and the ungulate; however, there was no trace of 'Ole Mousie or me. He stared at the gap for a few moments and finally saw the cow lying on her side on the ground with all four legs sticking straight out. He couldn't see me anywhere, but he could still hear me yelling for help.

Dad had been in the backyard of the house working on the lawnmower and had heard me yelling and screaming. He came running toward the barn thinking that Lewis and I were fighting with each other again and that Lewis was trying to "kill" me. We were always trying to "kill" each other. As brothers do, we were always fighting each other; but let someone else try to hurt the other, that was a horse of a different color. Then all hell would break loose against them.

When Dad saw Lewis and not me, he started yelling as he ran to the barn, "Where's your brother? What have you done to him?"

Lewis yelled back with a degree of indignation, "I haven't done anything to him; I don't even know where he is!"

When my dad reached my brother, they determined that the yelling and screaming were coming from the vicinity of the gap on the hill above the barn. As Dad and Lewis ran up the hill toward the gap, Dad saw 'Ole Mousie lying on the ground. Once they were close enough they could see my legs sticking out from underneath the fallen animal.

Fortunately for me, there was a depression in the ground where the Guernsey cow had fallen when she pinned me beneath her. The minute my dad and brother got to us, Dad asked me if I was alright. When I affirmed that I was not hurt, he and Lewis started to laugh. The more I protested the harder and louder they laughed.

Ultimately they began to try in earnest to get me out from underneath that drunken cow. At first, they were unsuccessful. My jeans kept getting longer and longer, but I wasn't coming out with them. I was **really** pinned beneath that 'ole heifer. Finally Dad got Mousie by the halter and pulled her head while Lewis tried to roll her off the top of me. My brother didn't have enough strength to budge her. He and Dad traded places. They were able to move 'Ole Mousie just enough that I could wiggle my way inch by inch out from underneath her. I wasn't hurt save for my pride; because it was my pants that were rescued first.

* * * * * *

Several years ago my parents took my wife and me back into the hollows by Snake Creek where my dad had grown up and where he and Mom had spent their honeymoon night and the first year or so of their married life. Mom was fifteen and Dad was two weeks shy of being eighteen when they recited their vows. They were mere children and didn't have the money to go anywhere for a honeymoon.

We turned onto a gravel road that was extremely rough because of the deep ruts cut into it. The road and its shoulder were too narrow for guardrails. Near the end of this road my dad's parents once lived in a log home, and that's where my parents spent their first night together as man and wife. As our car crept slowly around the sharp curves on the bumpy gravel road, Mom pointed out the narrow stream that ran swiftly along far below the edge of the state maintained road. The water tumbled over and over, slashing its way down through the middle of the narrow hollow, and tunneling its way through a culvert under the highway. Once on the other side of this paved road, the waters of the branch mixed into a larger stream known as Snake Creek, and together they slowed down and continued nonchalantly through a wide meadow to unknown destinations.

Mom told Charlotte and me that after the marriage ceremony she and Dad went up this same narrow county road, and before they could reach my grandparents' house darkness had overtaken them. It had been raining for several days and the narrow stream beside the dirt road had turned into a raging torrent. The flooding waters from that small branch filled the entire hollow below the banks of the rutted out road. By the time they had turned onto the gravel road the rain had stopped and a deep purple sky had begun to peer out from behind mounds of white puffy clouds. The light from a full moon and from billions of stars overhead made their intrusions into the velvet blackness. Reflections of their light off the crests of the rushing water made it appear that the currents were leapfrogging over the rocks that stuck up out of the water. Mom said that the glimmer emanating from the light of the moon and the stars resembled the eyes of monsters and she became frightened. By the time they reached the log cabin that was home to Grandpa and Grandma Vass at the upper limits of the road, Mom was literally trembling.

Dad took her one suit case from behind the seat of his Model-T, swept Mom off her feet, and carried her over the muddy front yard to the threshold of what would be their home for the next year.

The circumstances were not ideal for the start of married life, but somehow they survived and moved forward. Mom told us children that when she and Dad lay in bed at night, they could see stars twinkling through cracks in the ceiling of their bedroom. On some mornings when they awakened, the four or five quilts that covered them to keep them from freezing in their sleep would be overlaid by an inch or two of fresh fallen snow. My sister, Theoa, and my wife's eighty-three year old dad could relate to this. Theoa is eleven years older than I am, but having grown up in a similar environment, she could relate.

My wife's father, Chuck, had grown up under the same kind of conditions in Danville, Virginia. When he was barely a teenager, his father was decapitated while trying to save someone from being pinned between two railroad cars in the process of being coupled together. Chuck's mother was bringing his father lunch and witnessed the whole incident. She later spent time in a special hospital trying to recover from that dreadful incident.

Chuck grew up very poor, had to survive the Great Depression, and certainly could still remember the tough times and the cold winter nights when he didn't get warm until he was already in bed for a while.

It is intriguing to think of awakening to a blanket of snow upon your bed covers. I know that awakening in the morning under blankets that had been heated the night before certainly would not be the same as awakening under blankets covered with fresh fallen snow. Everyone has their own moments to ponder and reminisce about times like these.

Chapter Four

Saber Rattling

Dad was a foreman mechanic at the hosiery mill in the town where our family shopped and Lewis and I attended school. Many times my brother and I would accompany Dad when he went in on Saturday to repair a broken knitting machine. The cleaning crew, Dad, Lewis, and I would be the only people there. The mill was open only five days a week, so Dad would go in to do required maintenance when the machines were shut down. Lewis and I would tag along and have the run of the place to play hide and seek, or cops and robbers, or any other game we could invent. The possibilities were limitless in a building twice the size of a football field.

Dad had to quit attending school after the third grade; he went to work to help his family survive. His first job after he and Mom were married was as a knitting machine operator at the hosiery mill in Hillsville.

My father was a quick learner. The machine he operated was about ten feet high, ten feet wide, and fifty feet long. It had millions of working parts, and while he manned the machine on his shift, he studied its movements and how it worked. One day, one of the machines broke down so badly that the management team and mechanics sent over from Germany decided not to repair it, but scrape it. After the management team had left and the mechanics had gone back to Germany, Dad went to his boss, Mr. Fry, and asked if he would give him a shot at repairing the hosiery machine. Mr. Fry's initial reaction was to laugh at Dad. "If you think you can fix this monstrosity," he said, "go at it. But, do it on your own time. If you cannot make this thing work within two weeks, it goes for scrape metal."

As if he had been given the position of headman, Dad said, "Thank you, Mr. Fry. I will make this thing work."

When Dad finished working his regular hours each day, he worked on that machine, he worked on it over the weekend as well. Once my father had determined the problem, that's when he discovered that there were no replacement parts for the broken ones. That was why the decision had been made to scrap the machine in the first place. He took measurements and wrote down all the necessary information.

Working in the machine shop at the plant, he made the replacement parts needed to repair the machine. At the end of the day on Friday, the last day he was given to fix the problem, Dad replaced the broken pieces and turned on the machine.

Mr. Fry heard the thrashing sound of a working machine and came down from his office to the plant floor. He stood there for a few minutes watching my dad run off a dozen pairs of nylon hose. Approaching my dad, he yelled over the loud noise made by the machine, "Cut her off, Carbin!" After Dad had shut down the hosiery machine, Mr. Fry said, "So you did it! You fixed a machine that couldn't be fixed. How did you do it?"

Dad explained to Mr. Fry that there was one part that was broken in two and another part that was worn so thin that it wouldn't engage the opposing part when it came near. He told his boss that he had removed both parts and had made replacements in the plant workshop. Needless to say, Dad's boss was very impressed.

About two months after my father had shown his boss what he could do, Mr. Fry called my dad into his office. With Mr. Fry was one of the executives from Germany. They both complemented my dad on his initiative and for having saved a very expensive machine from the scrap heap. In spite of my dad's third grade education, the executive from the home office offered him the position of foreman-mechanic in charge of machinery maintenance. Of course he accepted and retained that position until the plant closed many years later.

The scrap metal that could not be reused was thrown into a pile behind the plant building. When the scrap heap grew sufficiently large, a salvage company was called to come and haul it away. Lewis and I liked to rummage through the scrap heap to find items that we could either make into something to play with later or things that we could play with while we were with Dad at the hosiery mill.

One particular Saturday we were rummaging through the pile of discarded steel rubble and found five foot long steel rods that were about the diameter of a radio antenna that cars used to have. We pulled two of these rods out of the pile and took them into the plant and asked Dad if we could take them home with us. Of course he agreed. Taking his car keys we placed the steel rods into the trunk of his Studebaker and continued playing in the vast mysterious building until Dad had finished his machine repairs and was ready to go home.

After church services the following day, Lewis and I changed into our play clothes as quickly as we could and hastened out to the workshop at the rear of the house. With his Tree Brand pocket knife Lewis began to whittle out a couple of wooden handles from two by two pine strips to go onto one end of the steel rods. While he whittled

I cut the rods down to three-foot lengths. I ground one end of each steel rod to a sharp point on the shop grinding wheel.

Lewis put his shoulder to my rear end and hoisted me up so I could climb into the attic of the shed where Mom had stored her extra Venetian blinds. I handed one of the bundles of blinds down to my brother. Holding onto the rafters I swung down to the floor of the workshop. Lewis removed one of the blinds from the bundle, clipped the cord that held each blind strip onto the whole, and removed a couple of two-inch-wide metal strips. He curved the Venetian blind strip around his fist to measure for proper length and then cut two of the strips into lengths of eight inches. After punching a hole into one end to slip over the steel rod, Lewis tacked the other end of the flat metal to the end of the handle he had carved out.

Eureka! There they were: foils, but without the knobs on their ends to prevent injury. In the hands of two pre-teens were instruments of death. We were so very proud of the "swords" that we had just made. For a few minutes, we crossed swords to hear the ring of metal against metal. We should have known that all would not end well.

At one point during our very first duel, I made an unexpected lunge with my foil and buried the point deep into the door of the outbuilding in front of which we were fencing. We had to stop our "play" so that we could work the rod up and down enough to free the point.

It didn't occur to us that we were playing with something that could maim and cause injury; that we were playing with fire, but fire is another subject for later.

After we freed the foil from the maple door we continued dueling. For five or six glorious minutes, Lewis and I crossed our homemade swords, reveling in the ringing sound of the clashing metal. Our moves seemed to have been choreographed; he would zig and I would zag. As we circled each other, we sized each other up for the "kill." I lunged toward my brother that took him totally by surprise. We truly never intended to hurt one another; it was simply that Lewis failed to zig when I zagged. The end of the pin-point steel rod found its mark between the forefinger and thumb of Lewis' right hand. The cold steel went deep and became lodged between two of my brother's wrist bones. I was just as shocked as he was.

I immediately let go of the handle of the homemade fencing piece and took a couple of steps backwards. The foil hung down from my brother's hand and swung back and forth like the pendulum of a grandfather clock. We stood there frozen in time, unable to move. With our mouths hanging limply open, we stared at the dangling foil. Keeping my distance, I finally leaned in and took hold of the handle and with a yank freed the sharp point from between the two wrist bones. Not one drop of blood came out. Instead, a clear fluid oozed out from the gaping hole.

Lewis looked up from staring at his hand and glared at me. Looking at my eyes, he surely saw my shocked expression. Taking full advantage of his confusion, I dropped my weapon to the ground, whirled around, and headed for the one-acre patch of pines in which we played and had most of our toys (weapons) stored. Gathering rocks as I ran, I stuffed them into the pockets of my jeans. My brother remained frozen in place from the shock of what had just happened.

When my pockets started to bulge at the seams, I took off my tee shirt. Using it as a carry-all, I filled it with rocks as well and headed for the single white pine tree that stood in front of a black pine forest. The top limbs of that white pine tree stuck out horizontally from being used as a nesting place in our play over the past couple of years. I climbed clear to the top of the pine tree and settled in with my stockpile of stone "missiles" ready for battle.

The realization of what had happened finally hit Lewis. He was wounded; I had done it and had run away. Clearly it was time for retaliation. There was not even a red badge of courage, as the gaping wound surrendered not one drop of blood.

It was about three o'clock in the afternoon of a typical summer day. The sun was up, the cattle were all lying in the shade, chickens were strutting about in the barnyard, and Mom and Dad were taking a siesta. Lewis ran to the base of the twenty foot rosin-soaked tree and grabbed hold of the first rung of branches to pull himself up.

I threw a stone missile down that hit him on the left shoulder. It stung enough to cause him to let go of the limb. Again he tried to pull himself up and again I threw a stone missile that hit him on the other shoulder. Each time Lewis tried to get past the first rung of limbs, I repelled him by the rocks I threw straight down at him. It didn't take but a few hits for Lewis to realize that getting to me at the top of that tree was not going to happen. I had positioned myself too well and had sufficient ammunition.

He considered his options and decided to let it go and get his revenge another time rather than continue to be pelted with rocks from above. He let go of the bottom limb and walked slowly back to the house. Knowing full well that by not saying a word and not swearing some oath of revenge, I would be haunted by fear and frustrated by the uncertainty of when and how he might retaliate.

Afraid to come down, I stayed in the top of that pine tree until it was almost dark. Lewis, on the other hand, went into the house, lay down on his bed, and took a little nap.

I was half sick from worrying about what I had done to my sibling's hand and the consequences that were sure to follow, to say nothing of the fact that I was being slowly but surely baked in the summer sun.

Sometimes it's the unknown versus the known that drives us crazy. As I recall, Lewis actually did nothing to me. It was enough that I harbored the fear that he would catch me unawares and then let me have it!

This was not an uncommon occurrence. Many times Lewis promised to do me in and never followed through. I think that that was much worse than if he had simply beaten me up or forced me to do all his chores.

It was almost dark before I dared come down out of that tree. I'm sure Mom wondered why she had to call me to come in for supper since my brother was already in the house. After all, we were always playing together on Sundays after church.

Even though it appeared that Lewis had allowed bygones to be bygones, something happened a few weeks later that caused me to think that "this was it." Sweet revenge was about to take place.

I had been in the "white building" behind the house. It was called the "white building" because it was not only painted white, it was the only shed, barn, or storage building that we had on the farm that had been painted any color. Except for the "white building," the cinder block barn, and our white shingled house, all the other buildings were a natural aged grey wood color. The "white building" was actually the tool shed and workshop. The door to the shed was set about a foot above the ground. When anyone entered or exited the building they had to step over this threshold. However, as children most often will do, when Lewis or I exited the "white building", we would step on the threshold and spring out into the yard in front of the door. On this one particular occasion, however, when I came out of the "white building," instead of bounding off the threshold like usual, which would have put my head above the lentil over the door, I simply stepped over it. That's when I heard a 22 caliber bullet go "zap" into the three inch wide pine door casing over my head. When I looked up, I saw my brother standing by the carport holding Dad's single bolt action 22 caliber rifle in his hands. His mouth was hanging open; his eyes were wide. He stood there planted to the ground like some oak tree. Shaken to my foundation I screamed at him, "Are you crazy? What are you doing?"

At first he struggled to speak, but managed finally to respond weakly, "I was preparing to shoot at some black birds on the power line going to the shed. When I pulled back on the bolt of the rifle it didn't hold. It slipped and the gun fired. I am so sorry! You're alright, aren't you?"

Piqued, I responded angrily, "Yeah, no thanks to you."

It was a miracle that he missed me. For some reason I didn't spring off the top of the threshold like I normally would have. Otherwise, the discharged twenty-two would have caught me right between the eyes.

I didn't know Jesus as my Lord and Savior at that time of my life, but I'm positive that Lewis did. He fell to his knees and must have said, "Thank you Jesus" a dozen times.

I know Lewis really didn't mean to shoot at me. I know that now, but at the time I wasn't so sure. Once again God intervened to spare one of our lives and save the other from grief. He was keeping us for greater things to come.

I laugh about it now, comfortably knowing that blood is thicker than water. No matter how much we might have ever been angry at one another, this family would always have stood up for and protected one another in the end. That's what family is all about.

Chapter Five

Snakes that Wink and Rattle Their Teeth

When Lewis and I were about thirteen and ten years of age respectively, we both received Boy Scout hatchets and hunting knives for Christmas. When spring arrived we attached the holsters that held the hatchet and knife to our belts, packed apples and peanut butter and jelly sandwiches in back packs, and told our mother that we were going for the day to play in the black pine patch behind the house. She agreed to our plan, never suspecting that her two little darlings were off for bigger adventure. We knew that she would be watching as we trekked our way to the entrance of the black pine forest, so we made nice and blew her kisses up until the time she would no longer be able to see where we were going and what we were doing. We went directly into the front of the wooded area, disappeared into the midst of the thickness, and went straight out the back side on our way to Little Reed Island Creek.

Little Reed Island Creek did not come close to Dad's property. Once we had reached the far boundary of our farm, not too far from the collapsed farm house on the Laury Farm, we were over a mile from our home. From there we followed a shooting stream that went through rock crevices, tumbled over three to four foot falls, and continued downward until the little rushing branch of water disappeared into the larger stream. All along that narrow branch were pools of water that were never any wider than four feet across, but they contained wild Speckled Mountain Trout. These native fish migrated up this tiny branch from Little Reed Island Creek and expelled their eggs. Tree limbs that had fallen across the small stream acted as dams that created these small pools of water. Whenever we passed by these pools we invariably would see fish dart across to the other side.

When we had the time, we would dig trenches to drain the water from the ponds and pick up one or two eight to ten inch Mountain Trout left behind flopping about on the mud bed.

There was one occasion when we didn't take the time to drain one of these pools. I stuck the barrel of Dad's 22 into the water and pulled the trigger. My intent was for the blast to burst the air bladder of the fish hiding underneath a fallen tree branch. With a ruptured air bladder the fish nearest the explosion would float to the surface of the water.

This time however, the back pressure of the water split the barrel of the rifle from its tip upwards four to five inches. That's why my father's 22 caliber rifle was a little shorter than other similar rifles.

Using a hacksaw, my brother cut off the split end of the barrel. He then drilled a hole into the top of the shortened barrel and inserted a screw. After filing the screw to flatten its sides, Lewis mounted the rifle on a fence post and drew a bead on a hand drawn target that he had attached to a bail of hay. He fired the gun and checked the target. After filing down the screw a millimeter, he fired the gun again and checked the target. He repeated this over and over until the rifle was as accurate as any gun with factory installed sights. However, that was a different period in time when shortening a rifle barrel was still legal.

Lewis and I arrived at Little Reed Island Creek around nine thirty in the morning. There was a swinging bridge that afforded a way to the other side of the river. The bridge was attached on our side of the water to a huge tree that leaned out over the bank of the river and to a smaller, yet substantial tree, on the other side. Near the south edge of Little Reed Island Creek a solid rock wall rose to a height of over thirty feet. Between it and the water's edge was an old logging road that was overgrown with elderberry, blackberry vines, poplar, alder, willow, birch, and hazel saplings In the base of the cliff was a shallow cave that went back only a few yards. On the floor of the cave were the bones of numerous small animals that had been caught and consumed by foxes, weasels, mink, and even bears that were just passing through. We could see that in times past hunters had spent the night in this natural shelter. Mixed with the bones on the floor of the cave were heaps of charcoal and partially burned kindling, beer cans, and sardine and potted meat cans. The ceiling of the cave had been blackened by the smoke of camp fires.

What child does not naturally like to climb? Scaling these cliffs was an adventure that could not be passed up. Lewis and began our climb to the top of the granite wall. Once we were about half way up, however, the rock wall turned into an overhang and could not be broached without special climbing equipment. To reach the top of the rocks, we had to make our way laterally to the side of the cliff, and from there crawl on our hands and knees beneath mountain laurel up the steep moss-covered ground We didn't notice that the moss was very spongy and full of holes.

I was leading the way up the side of the cliff. Without warning to my brother who was bringing up the rear, I stopped suddenly.

"Why did you stop?" Lewis asked.

Instantly wet with sweat, I responded weakly, "Don't move, I 'm eye to eye with a snake. I'm dead serious, Lewis, don't move a muscle. I'm face to face with a coiled copperhead, no more than eighteen inches from my nose."

Lewis backed away from me slowly to give me some wiggle room. Without making any sudden move, I inched my way back out of the strike zone. There was no doubt in my mind that God was in charge of what was going down. Copperheads so poised would not let you retreat without striking, but this one did. I reached around and removed the new Boy Scout hatchet from the holster attached to my belt. Taking careful aim, I threw the miniature axe.

"Oh great," I groaned.

Not knowing what had just happened, Lewis stuttered and asked me in a whisper, "What...what happened? Did...did you get him?"

"No," I answered in disappointment. "The hatchet missed him by no more than a cat's whisker and now it is sticking in the tree beside of the snake."

When the hatchet missed its mark and stuck into the scrub pine, the copperhead snake struck at me and recoiled like a leather whip being used by a cowboy showman to remove a cigarette from an assistant's mouth. Fortunately, Lewis and I had backed away just far enough.

"I think it's time to get out of here," I squawked.

We started backing up in tandem as quickly as we could in the thick mountain Laurel. Limbs were snapping at the skin of our exposed arms and branches kept grabbing for our shirt sleeves. My baseball cap got snatched by a limb that had been bent backward by my brother's butt as he crawled back down the hill. I just let it go. It was more important to get as far away from that serpent than to have an old worn cap.

Excitedly, I screeched, "Faster, faster, this black soggy moss is full of snakes!"

Not understanding what I had just said, my brother yelled back to me, "What did you say?"

"Snakes! Snakes! Snakes! Snakes are poking their heads up from the holes in the moss as we go over them. Go! Go! Go!' I screamed. "Get the heck out of here!"

I was backing up so fast that my rear end was pushing against my brother's face. I was yelling at him all the while, "Move it! Move it! Get out of here or we will both be bitten!"

I never moved so fast on my knees, and in reverse, in my entire life. By the time we had reached the overgrown logging road at the base of the rock cliff, our shirts were ripped and torn, both our baseball caps had been left behind as sacrifices to the Mountain Laurel, our hair was matted with leaves and twigs, and little wriggly trails of blood dotted our bare arms, necks, and faces.

We flopped onto the logging road and laid flat of our backs, taking in large gulps of air. Our chests were moving up and down in exaggerated expansions and contractions. Finally, I was able to say to Lewis, "I am stinging all over."

Between gulps of air, he replied, "Me too!"

I propped myself up on one elbow and asked, "You don't suppose we got bitten, do you?"

Lewis frowned and answered, "I don't know. I think all our stinging is due to the scratches, but I can't be certain."

My brother reached into his right hip pocket and removed an old wrinkled yellowish handkerchief that Mom always made him carry in case his nose might be runny. Of course it was unused; everyone knows that boys wipe their runny noses on their shirt and coat sleeves. He spit on the rag and began wiping away the streaks of blood on his arms and I did likewise with my own unused handkerchief. We then inspected each other, looking for the tell tale double dots that would be the bite marks left by fangs.

"Thank you, Lord," we said almost in unison. There were no bite marks, just lots of scratches and puncture wounds from broken twigs. We didn't bother to untangle our hair and remove the twigs and leaves; we were boys.

"What time is it," I asked?

Neither one of us carried a watch. Fortunately it was a cloudless day following a week of heavy rainfall. Lewis studied the sky for a moment through branches of alder and poplar and water oak that hung over the logging road.

"It must be between ten and eleven o'clock," he offered. "We left the house this morning at eight-thirty. It's been no more than a couple of hours since then and besides, the sun isn't straight up overhead of us yet. So, I would say, ten thirty."

"Great! We still have most of the day left to play," I said gleefully.

"Why don't we cross the river on the swinging bridge and go to the hill behind old man Crowder's cabin?" Lewis asked.

"We'll have to go way around his home," I responded thoughtfully. "That old man is strange. He might shoot us or something."

"He won't bother us if we don't bother him," my brother retorted confidently. "Besides, maybe we can sneak around his house and make like a bear and scare him so he won't come out."

"You know what, Lewis?" I remarked incredulously, "You're crazy. That's when the old man would come out for sure, and have his gun with him. I say we just be smart and make a wide path around his place."

Lewis reluctantly agreed. He still thought it would be funny to scare the old man; but he yielded to his easier-to-scare younger brother.

Because of the week long rains, Little Reed Island Creek had swollen to a raging river that had left its banks. Part of the meadow that we planned to cross had been underwater the day before, but the river had retreated to just outside its banks.

The swinging bridge was normally six or seven feet above the surface of the water, but was now submerged in about six inches of water in the middle where it sagged to its lowest point. The end of the bridge on our side of the river had its two two-inch ropes tied around the belly of the huge water oak tree. The roots of that massive tree were as large as a man's thigh and ran like the tentacles of an octopus over the surface of a gigantic granite boulder that stuck out over the river's edge. We had perched on this rock many times over the years fishing for chubs, catfish, and an occasional Speckled Mountain Trout that had returned to the river from the branch that went all the way to the back of Dad's farm.

We climbed to the top of the lichen-encrusted rock to where the ropes that held the bridge were tied. Lewis insisted that I go first out onto the swinging bridge. Initially I was very suspicious and certainly hesitant. After all, we did have a history of questionable antics, but my brother convinced me that since he was older and bigger, he would be able to hold the ropes tightly and keep the bridge from swinging. I knew that as far as the bridge was concerned, it was safe. However, I should have known that Lewis had his own agenda.

As soon as I had reached the middle of the bridge where the water of the river ran over its wooden planks, Lewis started yanking up and down on the ropes that supported the whole structure. He knew it was not nice, but my screaming and yelling made it worthwhile. After what was actually only a moment, but seemed an eternity for someone who was so frightened, he stopped yanking on the ropes and actually held onto them tightly so without further harassment I could make it to the other side.

When I reached the other side, I jumped from the bridge onto more stable ground, turned toward my brother, and started screaming at him, "Are you crazy? Why did you do that? You know that I could have fallen off the bridge and drowned!"

He couldn't believe I even asked that question! The answer was so simple: because he wanted to scare me. That was so obvious, as was his delight in torturing me.

There is an unwritten code by which bigger and older brothers have to abide. There are "rules" for goodness sake! Rule number one: if you are the older and bigger brother (and I think that bigger has to go along with older), you must inflict terror upon the younger and smaller brother. The senior brother must intimidate at all times, letting the younger brother know that because of his age and superior size, he is always in charge. Being the oldest also naturally makes him smarter and better looking. Finally, because the eldest is the one to appear in the family first, Mother loves him best. End of story. So when I asked the questions: "Are you crazy and why did you do that?" There was hardly any cause for response. "Older and bigger" was all that was needed to have been said.

Lewis walked across the rickety swinging bridge without hesitation. He knew that I would not do to him what he had just done to me. It was the rule of the big brother in play here.

Once we both made it to the other side of the river, and in order to not be detected, we headed in a wide swath around old man Crowder's log cabin that sat dead center of the meadow. When we had climbed to an area that overlooked his house, we came across a stone marker that had been planted halfway up the side of the hill. The lettering on the stone was hard to read because of the gray-green lichen that covered it. However, we were able to make out the letters: E-t-h—C---d—r, and remnants of a date: 19--.

We gasped when we realized that the name on the stone was more than likely Ethel Crowder, old man Crowder's missing wife. Stories had circulated about Mr. Crowder's wife disappearing a few years earlier. Mrs. Crowder and her husband walked from their home here in the meadow by Little Reed Island Creek to the nearest store to take eggs, blackberries, fresh vegetables, and chinquapins to exchange for staple goods. This country store was about three miles down Route Fifty-eight from the store where our own family shopped for staples and where Lewis and I waited for the school bus.

One day, Mr. Crowder came into the store without his wife. When asked if she were ill or anything, Mr. Crowder's only answer was, "No."

Once a week for years, he and his wife had gone to the store together. Never once did he ever give an answer to why she had stopped coming with him, or if she were alright, or even if she were still alive. Rumors circulated unfounded and unanswered as often they do. One rumor that circulated was that his wife had developed pneumonia and because old man Crowder didn't believe in wasting money on doctors, she not only did not recover from the infection, she had died.

Not against the law then, but certainly against human conscience, old man Crowder supposedly had placed his wife in a used fertilizer sack and had buried her remains somewhere on their property. He had been overheard at one time saying that she was where she could keep an eye on all that they owned.

The slope of the hill on which we stood overlooking the Crowder's log home was relatively steep. Above us were outcroppings of rock slides and enormous granite cliffs with shallow caves sticking out above a mélange of black scrub pine, spruce, and hemlock, and a miscellany of poplar, oak, black gum, and wild crab apple trees. Briers and thistle, wild strawberries, Queen Anne's lace, daisies, black-eyed Susans, dandelions, and cockleburs grew on the ground in soil that was mostly barren of nutrients. Patches of rust colored moss that thrived in the shadows of the rocks and trees thrust up their tall vascular stems, loaded with spores ready for the firing. At the base of the hill was a grassy down covered in heather with crowned, wiry leaves and racemes of light purple, pink, and white flowers.

Climbing to this location had been difficult, for the air was heavy and thick with white downy tufts of pollen thrust off from mature dandelions and thistles and fine yellow powdery pollen that had recently been dispelled from the pine trees. Tiny twirling "helicopters" that had been launched from the tall, slender maple trees that grew in a ring around the middle of the hillside were carried on the wind currents created by heat rising up from the surface of the rocks. Gnats and flies and mosquitoes bombarded our every orifice, many of which became stuck in the sweat on our faces and necks. Bumble bees collided with blossoms of flowering clover, and honey bees nuzzled up to the pestles of flowering dogwoods, picking up pollen on their hairy legs and transporting it from flower to flower to fulfill God's agricultural program. To the left of the gravesite was a granite rock slide that ran all the way from the top of the hill to its bottom.

While we stood gazing at the marker the sound of limbs snapping underfoot, rocks being kicked about, and heavy breathing came to our ears. Lewis and I were startled from staring at the gravestone and we jumped as if being fired upon. Scrambling as quickly as possible, we ran to a nearby thicket of mountain laurel and crawled underneath to hide. We held our hands over our mouths to muffle the sound of our own heavy breathing. We hid none too soon for old man Crowder came up to the site of the newly discovered marker.

He was a short stout man in his late sixties that walked with his shoulders bent forward slightly. His head stuck out past the rest of his body and he had a significant hump on his back. Old man Crowder's totally white hair was thin and straggly and stuck out all around from underneath a brown felt fedora that he kept pulled down low over his ears. Several strands of hair hung limply in clumps past the collar of his faded blue work shirt. His black and grey eyebrows were so thick and unkempt that they created a canopy over his eyes. From underneath those hairy bushes and from the depths of black encircled dark wells, it was hard to tell if he even had eyes. That's probably why he frightened us children so much.

Like many elderly people with whom we had been acquainted, including our own fraternal grandfather, old man Crowder's everyday wear, summer or winter, was a worsted wool suit. Every time that I had ever seen the man, the jacket of his chocolate brown suit appeared to be a size too large and hung on him like a toga. The threads on the sleeves of his jacket were frazzled, and black flannel patches had been added to the elbows to cover the holes that had come about by wear. The flaps on the pockets of his jacket stood straight out because of all the "junk" the old man carried in them. Numerous stains from spilled soup and gravy, and dribbled juice from meats and coffee ran in streaks down the front of his lapels.

It was difficult to hold our breath and at the same time try to take in extra air to replenish our oxygen-starved lungs. Lewis and I kept our hands over our mouths and sucked in air through o-shaped lips and let the air out as slowly as possible so as to make as little sound as possible. Old man Crowder came up to the lichen-covered marker and stopped. He must have realized that the rocks and weeds surrounding the marker had been kicked about and trampled down and disturbed. He tilted his head and looked from side to side and up and down the hill. He stared for a moment at the grove of mountain laurel in which Lewis and I hid. We just knew that he knew that we were there. 'Is he looking right at us? Can he see us?' I wondered.

I was about to take off running when he finally stopped looking our way and turned his eyes down to the ground. He placed his left hand on top of the marker to steady himself as he knelt down on one knee. He brushed some loose stones aside and placed the broken-down double-barreled shotgun that he had draped over his right arm onto the ground to the side of the marker. Removing his hat he laid it on top of his gun, and took a bunch of wild flowers from the right pocket of his jacket and laid them down on the ground in front of the marker. He commenced mumbling words so softly that we were unable to make out what he was saying. After a few minutes he raised his head and looked up toward the sky. With tears rolling down his cheeks, he began to make sounds like some wild animal moaning over its dead mate.

For the first time in my life I had compassion for this man we had always been afraid of. My breathing had eased up. With our oxygen-starved lungs finally replenished, Lewis and I had settled down and had become calmer. Lewis must have felt that he needed to go down and console this old grieving man. He rose up from his squatted position in the laurel thicket, but I grabbed his arm and pulled him back down. I looked at him with eyes wide open and shook my head violently from side to side and said in a whisper, "What are you doing? Stay down and don't make another move."

I must have really scared my brother. My eyes were wild and I kept shaking my head in the negative. I was saying to him softly that that old man would kill us without a second thought. Lewis could not hear what I was saying; he kept shrugging his shoulders and whispering, "What?"

Finally, he made out my words, "He will kill us!"

Lewis became like petrified wood. He thought that I knew something he didn't and became more and more uneasy. I started to tremble. Lewis put his arm around my shoulder and pulled me tightly against him to keep me still. Looking through the forked branches of the laurel, we saw old man Crowder get to his feet, put his hat back onto his head, and pick up his shotgun. He reached into the right pocket of his vest and pulled out two shotgun shells. Placing them into the barrels of his gun, with the snap of his wrist he closed the barrels shut. After pulling the hammer of the right barrel back, he put the gunstock to his right shoulder and pointed the gun in our direction.

Lewis pulled me closer to the ground. We closed our eyes tightly together. Children imagine that if you don't see the person who is looking at you, they can't see you. If you can't see what is about to happen, then it won't happen.

We heard the sound of a shotgun discharge. The blast echoed up and down the hillside and birds flew from their perches in all directions. Feeling no pain, I was afraid that Lewis must be the one that had been hit. I opened my eyes, but saw no blood. Lewis still had his eyes closed tightly together. Tears started trickling down my cheeks. I inched even closer to Lewis and he whispered in my ear, "Don't make a sound! Don't even move!"

My heart was pounding in my ears; I could hardly breathe. From where Lewis and I crouched on the ground, I peered through the lowest limbs of the laurel and could see old man Crowder's worn and cracked leather brogans right in front of us. Reaching down to the ground in front of the laurel thicket, he picked something up, turned, and walked away. He started back down the hill toward his log home, leaving the tombstone behind, leaving us behind. I leaned up on one elbow and could see that he was holding a grey squirrel by the tail. He was swinging it back and forth by the side of his leg as he made his way back down the hill by the side of the rock slide.

I asked just above a whisper, "Lewis! Lewis! Are you alright?"

He finally answered me, "Yeah, are you?"

"I'm okay," I whispered.

"Then let's get the heck out of here," my brother said emphatically.

We scrambled from our hiding place and ran away from the laurel thicket, away from the lichen-crusted tombstone, distancing ourselves from old man Crowder. The meadow at the base of the hill became more and more narrow and the hillside that we ran north along became steeper and steeper. Finally we ran out of ground. The hillside had become almost completely vertical, dropping fast into the swollen river below us. Suddenly, my feet went out from under me on the slippery moss-covered rocks and I started to slide down toward the muddy waters of the swift moving river. Lewis grabbed one of my wrists with his left hand just in time. He held on tightly with his other hand to the base of a mountain laurel. I was literally hanging in mid-air just above the churning brown waters of Little Reed Island Creek.

Fear gripped us as much as when clothes cling to one's body when wet. I was turning one way then another like a caterpillar hanging by a silk thread over an open flame. My brother was holding onto me as best he could. He screamed at me, "Stop squirming and grab hold of something!"

"I'm trying to," I cried. "Every time I take hold of something it either snaps off or pulls out of the ground."

The soil had been loosened by a week of rainfall. Finally I was able to plant one foot onto the base of an alder that hung out over the edge of the creek. It held. Feeling some of the pull on his arm lessen, Lewis reacted by asking me, "Are you on something?"

"Yeah," I wheezed. "I'm standing on a branch that appears strong enough to hold me for now."

We took a moment to regain our composure and catch our breath. I literally stood on a four inch branch of an alder over the surface of a creek swollen more than five to six feet. White caps licked at my feet soaking my pant legs half way to my knees. I tentatively asked my older and wiser brother, "How are we going to get out of this mess?"

"Now that I can breathe and think," Lewis responded with assurance, "I believe we can climb straight up the hill from here. There's a ledge above us that will lead us to more level ground. Be sure to test every branch you take hold of or stand on to make sure it won't pull out of the ground or break off. As I climb and secure my place, I'll give you a hand to pull up."

"Okay," I mumbled nervously. "Let's get out of here and go home. I have had enough adventure for today."

"Me too," Lewis affirmed. "It will take us a couple of hours to get home anyway, barring any more mishaps."

Limb by limb, root by root, we climbed upward until we reached the top of an outcropping of granite rock. We settled down with our legs crossed like Indians sitting before a cozy fire and sat there for a few moments staring down at the muddy brown water that raced by below us. Reflecting on our adventures that day, we recalled seeing mountain trout dart hither and yon in the branch that ran from Little Reed Island Creek to the back of Dad's farm, relived crawling over a bog of copperhead snakes and coming nose to nose with one coiled for the strike, and reminisced about swinging on a bridge that had a swollen creek spit on its boards. We thought about how we had discovered the whereabouts of old man Crowder's long gone wife and how we had nearly been caught by this "murderous old man," how that dead squirrel could have been us, and how close we had come to sliding to our drowning death in the high waters of a creek made a raging river by a week of heavy rains. Tired from the day's adventures, but energized by our youth, we left that cliff overlooking the water and headed home by a circuitous route to avoid coming near old man Crowder's log home.

When we walked into the back door of the house, our mother asked us if we had had a fun day of playing in the pines. Like the little angels that we were, we answered in unison, "yes, Mom!"

We removed our soiled clothes and left them on the enclosed back porch to be taken to the basement where the washing machine set. While my brother was taking a bath, I returned to the back porch to ask Mom a question. Standing in the doorway that led from the porch into the kitchen I saw her picking cocker burls from the legs of my brother's blue jeans. From where I stood I could see the puzzled look on her face. She knew that there were no cocker burrs growing anywhere near the pines in the back of the house. Forgetting what I had wanted to ask her I backed away slowly, turned and quietly tiptoed through the kitchen to my room.

At the dinner table I fully expected Mom to have inquired about the cocker burrs, but she said not a word. She was like that! Lewis and I knew that she was never really fooled by the things we thought we had gotten away with. After all, mothers have this all-seeing eye, which can even detect what is going on behind them. She corrected us often for the things that were necessary for our moral and Christian upbringing, but playing out of bounds must have never bothered her that much.

* * * * * *

One Saturday afternoon Mom, Dad, and I were visiting with my brother and his wife at their home in Shawsville, Virginia. Lewis asked if I would like to go with him upon the hill behind his house to see if we could catch some groundhogs out of their dens. Some things never change, so of course I agreed.

The hill behind my brother's home started at the end of his backyard and rose up at about a thirty degree angle. Parts of the hill had good grass growing and could be mowed over with a tractor, but the majority lay in waste, growing mostly thistles and briers, and Queen Anne's lace, unmanaged fescue and rye grasses, and small scrub pine.

Lewis handed me a small caliber rifle that held about nine rounds while he loaded one of the many revolvers he owned. We went out the back door of his house and started up the hillside to look for the pesky varmints, which left large holes in the ground surrounded by mounds of dirt. These holes presented a danger to cattle and horses. The animals could unexpectedly step into the holes and sustain injuries, even break a leg. Besides, it was just great sport to try and nail one of these annoying critters.

Panting and puffing like the little steam engine that could, we finally reached the top of the hill some five hundred feet above the back of Lewis' house. We stomped the weeds and grass down and plopped ourselves upon the ground for a few moments to rest and catch our breath.

As we sat there we enjoyed a plethora of smells that came wafting to us on the humid summer air. We could recognize the smell of rotting wood from the fallen timbers that lay at the summit just to the south of us. Our olfactory senses were tantalized by the sweet smell of tulip tree blossoms and freshly mowed grass from nearby farms, the delightful aroma of heather and wild clover that grew abundantly on the nearby downs, the overpowering odors of wild dogwoods and Bradford pear trees, and the fresh smell of pine that was reaching the age of maturity at the Christmas tree farm on the hill nearby.

Bumble bees and honey bees picked up their burden of pollen as they buzzed purposefully between purple blooms of clover and the off-white blossoms of Queen Anne's lace. The other insects that are lively by day, the Swallow-tail and Monarch butterflies with their large, broad, brightly colored wings flitted from flower to flower, never seeming to stay long enough to accomplish any purpose.

God's creation buzzed and hummed, flitted and flirted, attracted and repelled, and demonstrated what a wonderful world He had created.

Once we were able to breathe normally again, we got to our feet and started to make our way around to the woods at the summit of the hill. From there we could get a better view of the area where the groundhogs had dug their burrows. We would be able to detect the holes in the ground by the yellow-brown mounds of dirt that surrounded them.

With his right foot high in the air to crush down the thistles and briers and cockle burrs that reached out for his pant legs, Lewis suddenly stopped in front of me. As if playing the children's game of "Freeze," he became as motionless as a bronze statue on the lawn of a museum. At first I thought he had spotted a ground hog out of its hole and wanted me to freeze as well, so I too stopped and became motionless. I moved my eyes from side to side very slowly, but I didn't see any groundhogs. Not having followed exactly in my brother's footsteps, I could see the side of his face. Lewis' right eye was blinking rapidly like someone who suffered with a tic. Tears broached the rim of his blinking eye and ran headlong down his cheek and dripped off his chin. He moved his lips, but there were no words. Something was definitely not right.

Not being able to withstand the pressure, I asked just above a whisper, "What is it? Have you spotted a groundhog?" Sweat began to build up on his brow and his hair that touched the collar of his plaid shirt became visibly wet. More loudly than before I asked, "What's wrong?"

My brother's lips continued to move up and down like the mechanical lips on a puppet, but he still was not making any sound. However, he slowly raised the barrel of his pistol from pointing toward the ground to pointing straight ahead and slightly downward. I still didn't get it, but without knowing what was happening, I stayed perfectly still. Growing up with someone produces an interactive knowledge whereby it is sometimes unnecessary to speak to know that silence is golden and remaining motionless is absolutely essential.

With the revolver at his waist, Lewis looked just like a Western gunfighter facing his foe in a shootout. He placed his thumb on the hammer and pulled it back. When he pulled the trigger, the noise of his 357 Magnum was deafening. Instantaneously with the explosion of the shell, Lewis brought his right foot that had been held in the air back and down as he ran backwards a few feet and screamed, "Snake!"

He didn't have to say that word but once. I was right back there beside him. His right eye was still blinking rapidly and he was stuttering the words, "Snake…snake, copperhead. I almost stepped down on top of them!"

With a wave of fear going up my back like an ice cycle being rubbed up and down my spine, I stammered, "The…them! What do you mean them? You only fired once, Lewis, what do you mean them?"

"I was about to step down on the one that was coiled and its mate was just beyond it," he answered.

We stood there for a few seconds collecting our wits, but we also knew we couldn't just stand there the rest of the afternoon. Slowly Lewis inched his way back on the mashed down weeds and grass to where he had seen the copperheads. I gave him support from behind…. way behind. Right where he had discovered the copperheads laid a partially coiled snake with his head blown off.

Now sweating profusely myself, I asked, "Where's the other one?"

Like a cosmic revelation, we said simultaneously, "Yeah, where is the other one?"

Our rapid movements seemed to be playing out in slow motion. We turned to face downhill and with only the soles of our shoes touching the very tops of the weeds and grass blades, we rocketed back down to the safety of the yard with the manicured lawn. Bent over at the waist and holding our sides to stop the hurting, we gasped for every molecule of oxygen that we could suck out of the hot, humid air of summer.

Lewis' wife, Betty, and our mom had been washing the dishes from lunch in front of the kitchen window and had witnessed our speedy retreat down the hill. They yelled for Dad, who had been watching TV in the den with my brother's two children, to join them. Something was up. They came into the backyard. Betty stood over us with her arms crossed and was the first one to speak, "What in the world happened up on the hill?"

Lewis told them about the copperhead snakes and that he had shot the one poised to strike, but didn't see what had happened to the other one.

"Lewis saw another snake, but I didn't," I chimed in, still sucking in extra air. "Our legs started moving without having to be told twice."

That's when it hit me how absolutely funny this had been and started to embellish the story a little to our parents and to Betty. I told them how Lewis had shot off the head of the snake from his waist (which he did), but that not once did his feet hit the ground on the way back down the hill. "He ran so fast," I said, "that I believe he actually ran on top of the grass."

Dad took the cue and said, "Wow! That's amazing!" Then he asked with a touch of sarcasm, "What did the snake do?"

My mind raced forward to think up something absurd, so I said, "Well that snake rolled his eyes back in his head and started to blink just as rapidly as Lewis' eyes had begun to blink. The snake pushed down its lower lip on one side, raised his upper lip to expose one fang, and started moving its mouth up and down smacking its lips together. He also produced a popping noise by rapidly thrusting its tongue against the roof of its mouth. The popping, sucking noise was in sink with its blinking eye. It appeared that Lewis and the snake were frightened equally. As far as I know, the other snake headed for a hole in the ground and was out of sight by the time Lewis discharged his pistol."

Dad asked me if I could demonstrate how that snake did his "smacking" noise. So I complied with his wishes by blinking my right eye rapidly and hanging my upper right canine over my lower lip. I made the popping sound with my tongue hitting against the roof of my mouth and the sucking sound by smacking my lips together.

By the time I had finished showing Mom, Dad and Betty the exaggerated antics of the copperhead snake, they were in fits of laughter. This was not the last of Lewis' or my encounters with poisonous snakes, however.

* * * * * *

I came home from college one Sunday afternoon to visit with my folks; but they were not at home. They were attending church somewhere in the area.

In those days where I grew up, no one locked the doors or the windows of their houses. People would leave their windows and doors open to let the cool breezes go in through the screens to keep their houses comfortable. When I realized that my parents were not at home, I went up the steps of the front porch, opened the screen door, and walked in.

I went to the closet beside the front bathroom, the one that had been added onto the house by enclosing part of the front porch, and retrieved Dad's twenty-two rifle from behind the closet door. Deciding to take a walk to the Laury Farm, I loaded a bullet into the twenty-two's chamber before heading out. The Laury Farm was a thirty-three acre farm on the backside of the hill behind my parents' home. My father had bought this scruffy piece of land five years earlier and had added it to his well-groomed farm.

Because it was one of those hot mid-August days, I determined to stay cool by wearing an old tee shirt, a pair of thin cotton shorts, and a pair of badly discolored Converse tennis shoes. By the time I got to the lowest part of the Laury Farm just past the old farm house, the temperature felt to be ninety degrees or higher. Down low in a meadow between two hills the air absolutely refused to stir.

To the right of the dilapidated farmhouse (two-thirds collapsed from neglect) set a log barn containing only two stalls. Large capped mushrooms and numerous unnamed weeds grew up through the musty straw that covered the dirt floor. Between the house and the barn grew grass lush and green because of an underground spring at the head of this small clearing. The springhead had not been cleaned out and channeled in years so the water spread out creating a marsh.

Climbing wild roses and blackberry vines overgrew the side of the house that faced away from the marsh and log barn. The part of the porch that surrounded the south and west sides of the farmhouse had fallen down. On the west side of the house the porch still stood head high. The bloated carcass of a Guernsey calf laid under the porch with half its face rotted off. It appeared that the calf had gone underneath the porch to take advantage of the shade but ended up being bitten by a copperhead snake.

Keeping one eye on the dead calf and the other on the lookout for snakes that might still be around the porch, I inched my way to the rear of the house. As I stepped from the ground to the top of a gigantic granite boulder sticking up out of the ground in back of the house, a chill came over me and ran up and down the entire length of my body. All the hair on my arms and legs stood straight up. One could liken it to an ethereal out-of-body experience.

I froze in place. Even though I was now standing on only one foot, I was able to maintain an uncanny balance. I had taken a step onto the granite boulder and my other foot was ten or so inches above the rock as I started to take the next step. Something or "someone" told me not to move. I looked down to see that, like Lewis, my next step would have been down on top of a copperhead snake, coiled for the strike.

I was carrying the 22 caliber rifle draped over my right arm, but it was not cocked. To boot, it was a single-shot pull-back bolt-action gun, which means that it would normally have required both hands to prepare the gun for firing. One would normally have had to hold the rifle in his left hand so that the forefinger and thumb of the other hand could pull back the bolt on top of the gun to "cock" the mechanism for firing.

The reason for explaining this is to show that God, as He has done so many times in both my brother's life and my own when we were growing up, took supernatural control over whatever situation in which we found ourselves. With the gun between the inside of my right arm and my right rib cage, I was somehow able to hold the rifle tightly enough against my ribcage with the underside of my arm to "cock" the firing mechanism with the forefinger and thumb of my right hand. With the same hand around the rifle and my index finger on the trigger, I raised the gun. This was the same gun that the bolt had slipped and fired over my head years earlier when Lewis was cocking it to shoot at black birds on a power line behind the house. This gun had a history of the plunger not holding when you pulled back the bolt to cock the hammer, but this time it did. This was just another example of how our lives continually fell under the protection of God.

Without being able to look down the barrel through the near and far sights, I pulled the trigger and "splat," right into the wide-open mouth of the copperhead went the hollow-point 22 caliber bullet. As the mortally wounded snake started to wriggle about, its mate some eighteen inches behind started to uncoil and slither down one of the many holes between the loose granite rocks that lay strewn about on top of the larger granite boulder. Putting my right foot down and taking a step backward off the flat granite boulder, I ratcheted the bolt that ejected the single shell casing and fumbled in my right shorts' pocket for more ammo. My hands were shaking so badly that I could hardly withdraw another shell and place it into the chamber of the single-shot rifle. I dropped three or four bullets before I was finally able to shove one into the chamber. With about half of the second snake's body in the hole and vanishing rapidly, I was finally able to reload and again "cock" the rifle. This time I did have the luxury of taking aim. I pulled the trigger and saw the hollow-point rip through the side of the retreating threat. Blood and fluid splattered all over the white and gray granite rock around the hole as that serpent disappeared from sight. It may not have been a visible kill like the snake that had taken the hit of the 22 in its mouth, but I can assure you that the companion snake could not have survived the wound to its side.

I don't know if there were other copperheads around or not. I don't even know how I came out of that meadow or when I did, but before I realized it I was about halfway home. Two-thirds of that mile home was uphill. My legs must have looked like those of the Road Runner in cartoons. They were churning so fast I am sure my legs resembled a blurred wheel. I did not stop running until I fell exhausted into one of the green Adirondack chairs on the front porch of Mom and Dad's house. I was still shaking and was wringing wet from panicked perspiration.

By the time I had completely calmed down, Mom and Dad returned home from church. They saw me sitting on the front porch, still "glued" to the lawn chair. After parking their car in the carport, Mom and Dad got out and came around to the front of the house where I sat. When they came upon the front porch, Dad was the first one to speak, "Well look what the cats drug in!"

I rose to greet them, and gave Mom a big hug. She pulled back from me and asked, "Why are you so wet?"

I told them the whole snake story and how I had shot the first one from the hip and the other by taking aim. Knowing that I must not have been bitten, considering that I had run a mile to home and was still alive, Dad asked me if the snake I shot in the mouth had blinked one eye, hung one fang over his lower lip and made a smacking, sucking sound with his tongue against the roof of his mouth.

I knew he was referring to the humorous description I had given to them a year earlier when Lewis and I had encountered the copperheads on top of the hill behind his house and had come flying down that hill into his backyard. We laughed about that one all over again.

Chapter Six

Spooks, Goblins and Other Scary Things

A good jumping off place to talk about ghosts and goblins and other assorted scary things is when you have finished talking about snakes, especially snakes that smack their lips and tongues and blink their eyes at you. I truly don't know whether they were the ones to initiate these gestures or whether they were simply mimicking my brother.

I don't recall whether the incident I am about to tell you happened the same year as the "Great Winter Storm" or not, but I was on my hands and knees pushing snow with my toy truck in the driveway about halfway between the house and the public highway. Any deep snow that had filled our drive had been removed, but there remained a thin white ice crusted powder that covered the dirt road like a stiff white blanket. It was about nine o'clock at night and the sky was alight with billions upon billions of stars, and the moon was full and smiled down on the earth from straight up overhead. The light of the moon and the stars lit up the whole night, being reflected off the ice-covered snow that covered the entire countryside. The Tonka truck with which I was playing was equipped with a snow blade. Making blubbering sounds to represent the sound of the laboring truck's engine, I was unaware that anyone or anything had approached me from behind.

The air was crisp but dead still, with not one molecule of air stirring. Without perceiving any sound, I sat straight up and arched my back. I could not have become more rigid if I had actually been frozen stiff. A chill came over me more profound than any chill that I had ever experienced from being cold. I was unable to move for at least two full minutes. Without changing my position I looked down at the snow covered dirt road in front of me. Extending a foot or two beyond me was a shadow cast by someone or something very tall. I turned around slowly and sat back on the top of the snow. What had been standing behind me, I now faced straight on. I stopped breathing. I couldn't swallow. My entire mouth became so dry that my tongue clung to the roof of my mouth and my teeth stuck to the inside of my lips. Standing there in the drive before me was a dark figure that must have been seven or eight feet tall. I am not exaggerating, for when one grows up on a farm they become very accurate in estimating heights and lengths and weights.

I managed to get out the words, "Who are you and what do you want?"

The dark figure that stood before me like some mirage did not say a word nor did it move. It was dressed in a very dark blue or black cape that cascaded all the way down to the snow. The cape was fashioned at the top into a hood that covered the intruder's head. I could not see a face. The moon was directly above the figure's head so that there were only dark shadows.

Finally, I rose to my feet with full intentions of running away; but as I started to get up, the ghostly figure in front of me retreated a couple of feet. We now both stood facing each other. As I started to slowly back away, the figure turned to face the hill to my right. It moved quickly to the wire fence that kept cattle out of the road when the field was being used for grazing in the spring and summer months. The fence that normally was approximately five feet high now appeared shorter, as it was covered halfway up by a bank of snow. The dark figure went straight to the fence and without climbing up and over, simply went over the structure. It seemed to have glided up to the top of the hill and disappeared underneath the tall white pine trees that bordered the south side of the family cemetery. I watched it all the way without running away. I couldn't run; it was if my boots had become stuck to the top of the snow.

Once the dark figure had disappeared from sight, the snow let go of my boots. I turned and ran like the wind back to the house. There were three steps that led up the porch to the front of the house, but I skipped all three. I leaped like a gazelle from the snow covered front yard onto the porch and in one continuous motion opened the front door, went straight to the sofa, and fell face down upon it.

My mother knew instinctively that something was wrong. She asked me what was going on, but I could not answer. My mouth was dryer than ever, my tongue was still stuck, and I couldn't talk through my heavy breathing. Eventually I managed to get out the words, "I saw something!"

With that concerned motherly voice, Mom asked me, "What did you see, baby?"

By this time my dad and brother had come into the room. They wanted to know what was going on. Mom answered them by saying, "Larry says he saw something."

My brother was the first to ask, "Well, what did you see? Was it a bear, a mountain cat, or maybe a flying saucer?"

Then he began to laugh at me. I was still breathing hard, obviously in distress. I must have looked like I had been frightened half to death. I couldn't believe he was making fun of me; but of course, he had not seen what I had seen.

I snapped at him through clenched teeth, "I saw something that looked just like the pictures of the Grim Reaper you see in books. I know that it was not of this world because it went up and over the fence without having to actually climb over it. Whatever it was then went straight up the hill to the graveyard and disappeared underneath the pine trees there."

Suddenly it wasn't so funny to my brother any more. Dad's curiosity was peaked and he asked me, "What do you mean this 'Grim Reaper' thing went up and over the fence without climbing over? Where did you see this?"

"About halfway to the highway," I replied, "I was playing in the snow with my truck and bulldozer when something real eerie happened. There was a shadow that covered me and I could see it on the ground in front of me because of the light of the moon. In spite of the fact that there is absolutely no wind tonight, I became chilled to the bone. When I turned around, that thing was standing in front of me. It had to be seven to eight feet tall."

"Seven or eight feet tall?" my brother mocked. "Are you kidding us?"

"No, I am not kidding," I stormed. "The fence that borders the road is five feet high and that thing stood two to three feet taller than the fence."

Suddenly the comparison I put forth struck a cord. Lewis stopped laughing. Mom turned to Dad and said, "Why don't you take a flashlight and your shotgun, and you and Lewis go with Larry back out there to see if you can find any trace of what he saw. Look at him! You can see that he hasn't made any of this up. Why, he's trembling all over. He's obviously been scared half to death."

I objected; I didn't want to go back out there. I knew that thing was not of this world, and I didn't see any need for me to return to that spot. But like a military operation being formulated, "General Dad" told "First Lieutenant Lewis" to get the shotgun and a hand full of shells and "Private First Class Larry" to get the flashlight off the top of the hot water heater and reassemble right where we were presently standing at nine hundred hours and fifteen minutes. Instinctively, I knew that there was no need for protests; the reconnaissance operation had begun.

Without hesitation, Lewis ran to the closet nearest the bathroom that had been added to the front porch. He retrieved the long-barrel twelve gauge shotgun from behind the inside door frame of the closet, and grabbed a handful of shotgun shells out of a box that set on the top shelf. With a display of disapproval unnoticed by anyone else, I got up slowly from the black Mediterranean sofa that Mom had decided that we needed back in the summer and moved with the speed of an old snail to the enclosed back porch to retrieve the flashlight. As directed, we reassembled in the den.

Of all the things that Dad could possibly have done to dismay me, he shoved me to the front and said, "Show us where you saw your 'Mr. Grim Reaper.'"

I thought to myself, 'Did you not see the look on my face? Did you not see that whatever that thing was scared me half to death and you want me to lead the way?'

Like a good soldier, however, I did as instructed and took the lead. I led Lewis and Dad back to the halfway point of our driveway and announced with timidity, "There's my truck and bulldozer. This is where 'the Thing' approached me."

Pointing the flashlight toward the ground, Lewis and Dad searched for signs of "that thing." The snow that was packed hard on the drive revealed no foot prints or any signs of disturbance beyond where I had been pushing the snow with my toy truck and bulldozer. Walking up to the fence, Dad shined the beam of light up the hill toward the family cemetery. There were no foot prints in the icy snow there either.

With reservation in his voice, Dad turned to me and asked, "Are you sure this is where you saw what you think you saw? Are you sure that you saw anything? Maybe the light of the moon and the stars being reflected off the surface of the icy snow produced shadows so that you thought that you saw a figure?"

"No Dad," I protested vehemently. I stamped my feet and insisted, "I was not imagining anything! There was something or someone out here!"

Lewis backed away quickly from the fence as if <u>he</u> saw what I had seen and summoned our dad, "Look here Dad! There's ice covering all the strands of wire on the fence except right here where Larry said that 'thing' went up and over."

They examined the fence in the light of the flashlight. All the strands of the wire in the fence at this point were void of ice. On the other side of the fence was a depression in the snow and in it were pieces of ice that had come off the strands of wire. However, the sunken area did not look like anything with any weight had come down on top of it. Dad looked at the wire in the fence and found that all the other strands were still covered by ice. He grabbed hold of the wire fence and shook it hard, but no ice fell from the wire. It was frozen too hard. The only way he could make the ice come off the stands of wire was to actually take hold of the wire and physically strip the ice away.

Much to my delight, Dad made an executive decision. He announced, "Let's go to the house and check more on this tomorrow when we have daylight."

After we were tucked into our bunk beds and the heated blankets had been thrown over us, Mom kissed Lewis and me on our foreheads and wished us goodnight before she left the room.

In a matter of minutes Lewis had fallen asleep. I, on the other hand, was left alone to face the creatures of the night. Three tall white pine trees and a solitary apple tree in which we had built a playhouse stood outside the window of our bedroom. The wind had begun to blow and I could hear it moaning as it swirled though the top limbs of the pine trees. Pushed by the wind, the limbs of the trees undulated back and forth, casting shadows onto the wall opposite my bed. Every time I peeped out from underneath the covers, I could see the shadows reaching for me. I had to stay awake and be on watch all night to make sure that none of the shadows were able to grab my brother or me and drag us out through the window. When I did finally drift off to sleep in the wee hours of the morning, I kept visualizing that hooded creature hovering over me. I had no doubt that he would grab me and carry me off to the graveyard.

Morning arrived none too soon. I had fallen asleep only for the last hour or two before the sun came up. I felt exhausted. Lewis and

I were awakened abruptly when we heard our mother yell from the kitchen, "Come to breakfast!"

Lewis bounded out of bed and grabbed his clothes lying across the bottom of his bunk bed and ran to stand over the grate of the furnace in the den to get dressed. Despite the cold in our room, I slowly got out of bed. I picked up my folded clothes that felt colder than the inside of a refrigerator, and stumbled through the bedroom door into the den. Lewis and his clothes were spread out over the grate showing no signs of sharing the heat or the space. This morning, however, I didn't even care. I went over and plopped down on the sofa and started putting on my icy cold jeans and socks. By the time I had put on my brogans, Mom called us to breakfast again.

When we finished eating our breakfast Dad got up from the table like the leader he was and said, "Come on boys! Let's go see if we can find Larry's spook."

My heart went up into my throat. I knew I must have turned a deeper shade of red for my mother asked me if I felt alright. I told her that I did. After we had donned all of our winter gear and pulled up our rubber boots, Dad started out the front door. I cried out, "Wait a minute! Aren't you going to take your gun?"

Dad stopped abruptly and turned around on one heel. He stared at me for a second and asked with incredulity, "Why? No creature is going to be out in the daylight." He paused and allowed himself to chuckle and then resumed, "Whatever you saw last night will surely be long gone, Larry. We're going to see if we can find out what you saw. After all, I don't want you to be afraid to play outside after dark."

I reluctantly bowed to his wisdom and the three of us "men folk" went out the front door. When we got to the spot in the fence where all the ice had been removed from the strands of wire, we climbed over and crunched our way through the deep ice-encrusted snow to the family cemetery at the top of the hill. On the way up we observed no detectable tracks in the snow whatsoever. About halfway, Dad said, "Unless this creature or person or whatever it was floated above the snow, it would have had to leave some tracks, and there are none."

I'm certain he could see the disappointment on my face. "But I saw it, Dad," I protested. "I'm telling you the truth."

"I'm not saying you're not telling the truth, Larry," he responded. "It's just that, except for the ice being gone from the wire…"

"And the depression on this side of the fence," I interjected quickly.

"And the depression in the snow on this side of the fence," he concurred, "there are no other evidences of anyone or anything coming up this hill."

When we reached the cemetery, Dad pushed hard on the chain-link gate, plowing the ice crusted snow ahead of it. We stepped through into the inner sanctum of the family graveyard. The snow and ice that covered the ground on this hill was less than a foot deep. The wind had come across the crest of the hill and had blown most of the snow into drifts further down the hill by the fence beside the driveway. The three of us stood perfectly still. The dozen or so graves were all covered by snow like the rest of the ground. However, three crude unlettered stones that marked the gravesites of three unidentified persons buried there were lying face down at the top of the gravesites. There was not one flake of snow covering the ground over those graves. The ground was bone dry and the grass was fresh and green as if it were spring.

Lewis was the first one to speak. He asked Dad, "Why are these graves not covered with snow and why is the grass over them green? Whose graves are these anyway?"

"I have no idea why they are not covered with snow like the rest," he answered. "No one knows who's buried in these plots. These stones were placed to mark the spot where three strangers were interred long ago, before your mother and I were even married.

"The story that I heard," Dad said, "was that a man and his wife and their baby were passing on foot through this part of the country many years ago and having no place to stay when night came, asked the Goads who owned the store across the road from this cemetery if they could spend the night. It was said that Mr. Goad didn't like the idea of strangers staying with him and his wife, but being a Christian man, didn't want to turn them away either. Beside the store was a metal building that was used to house fertilizer, sacks of chop for hogs, and bags of grain for cattle. The owner of the store told the couple that they and their baby could stay in that building for the night. By bedding down between the piles of bagged grain and chop, they would be very warm and comfortable. Mr. Goad told the couple they could have breakfast with them the next morning.

"That night the couple and their baby came down with a mysterious fever and died. The next morning when the couple didn't show up for breakfast, Mr. Goad went to the metal building to check on them. He banged on the metal door, but there was no response. He slid the door open and found the man, his wife, and their baby snuggled together between chop sacks. When he tried to wake them, he realized that they were dead.

"No one knew who they were; that's why the markers have no names written upon them"

"Let's go home Dad," I said. "These gravesites with green grass growing on the tops of them in the middle of winter scare me. I want to go!"

"Me too," my big brother added.

That was such a big deal. My brother would never, but never have admitted to being scared of anything. For him to indicate that he was scared in front of not only me, but Dad, was huge.

Dad agreed, "Okay, boys. Let's go. This is not making me feel very comfortable either."

We left the hilltop and went straight back down to the house and told Mom all about what we had seen. After that day, it was never mentioned again.

* * * * * *

At one point or another, all little boys decide to run away from home. There was a time when Lewis and I had decided to do so ourselves. I must have been seven or eight years old and Lewis ten or eleven. Mom had punished us for something that we most certainly deserved, but we were mad at her and her "dictatorship," and had announced our pending departure.

Lewis went to the linen closet and retrieved an old pillow case into which we placed a change of underwear and socks. We added a few ripe apples, a chunk of day-old corn bread, a Mason jar of canned sausage, several slices of cooked fatback, a few slices of American cheese, and one of the four sleeves of crackers from a box of Zesta saltines. That seemed sufficient for two boys leaving home with no plans to return.

Mom even held the door open for us as we left. She wished us well and said that we were always welcome to return. We assured her that we would not ever be coming back. She insisted that we kiss her goodbye, because if we were truly never coming home, she wanted to have the memory of kissing her two boys one last time. Reluctantly, we each gave her a peck on the cheek and took off.

We quickly made our way past the buildings behind the house, passed by the cinder block barn where the cows were fed and milked, and finally reached the top of the hill where we were able to disappear out of our mother's sight. We knew that she would be watching us from the window over the kitchen sink.

It was getting late in the day and we had already fed the cows, milked them, and turned them out to pasture. That was our job and we didn't want to run away from home until our chores had been taken care of. The whole purpose of running away, of course, is to make your mother worry, cause her to regret that she had ever punished you, and give rise to her coming to look for you with an apology on her lips.

We sat hidden on the top of the hill for a couple of hours. The sun had started to descend behind the tops of the mountains to the west and Mom had not yet called for us to come home. Feeling anxious over the fact that our mother may have been content to let us go, we got to our feet and walked to the west a hundred yards so that we would remain hidden by the barn. Keeping the barn between us and the windows of the house, Lewis and I came down from the hilltop to one of the buildings that sat directly behind the house.

There were three outbuildings: one was a small brick building that had once been a springhouse, but now was used to store burlap sacks of potatoes and canned goods, the "white building" that was the work and tool shop, and the third (the one in which we chose to hide) was a multipurpose building with four sections. Across the front of the building that faced the back of the house was a granary on one end where field corn was stored, a middle section where cured and salted hams were hung, and the other end was where the farm tractor and lawn mower were housed. On the backside of this building was an open front end shed that we had filled almost to the roof with surplus bales of hay.

When we got to this building, we climbed up the front of the bales of hay and crawled on top where there was just enough room under the metal roof for two small boys to hide. Even though darkness had come, we could still see quite well. The sky was cloudless and the August moon was three quarters full. It got to be around nine o'clock and Dad had not come home from working third shift at the hosiery mill. He went into work at three in the afternoon and would not get home until around eleven-thirty at night. Mom had still not called or come looking for us.

We had eaten the sausage and cheese and saltine crackers while sitting on top of the hill. We were hungry again and all we had left were the few pieces of fried fatback and the apples. So we ate them. For a little while longer we lay on our backs on top of the hay under the tin roof and whispered all kinds of nonsense to each other. We whispered to one another just in case Mom came looking for us, and we didn't want to miss hearing her if she were to call out for us to please come home.

There were movements and sounds everywhere. Heart-stopping shadows crept about, pausing for a few seconds at a time to glare at us. With every puff of wind a shadow with multiple arms and spidery fingers reached out in an attempt to snare an unsuspecting victim, but when the wind died so did the shadowy beasts. One dark creature came slivering over the top of the "white building," and tried desperately to escape the confines of its tin roof. It advanced relentlessly but just before breaking free, the summer breeze ceased and it retired to try again as soon as a new surge of wind came by. We were not sure if we were listening to the hooting of a barn owl or the noise created by ghosts. The cries of the crepuscular whip-poor-will were obvious warnings of the night lest anyone venture too far from the safety of those who were older and bigger and who could offer protection.

The cacophony of sounds of the night was broken by the sounds of grunting. Lewis grabbed me by the arm and pulled me close.

"What is it?" I asked nervously.

"Shush!" He instructed. Even my whispering was too loud. He leaned forward, cupped his hands around my ear and said so as not to let a sound escape into the night, "There's something down on the ground in front of us."

"What is it," I asked, more nervous than before.

"I'm not sure," he responded cautiously. "Stop talking so loudly."

"I'm not talking loudly!" I said with indignation.

Finally, Lewis placed his hand over my mouth and whispered into my ear, "Don't make another sound and I mean it. There's something down there and I don't mean some tree casting a shadow on the wall of the shed or on the ground."

It was so hard to breathe without making a single solitary sound. Lewis and I had being lying on our backs facing the tin roof, but now we flipped over onto our stomachs and stared out into the darkness. Something was coming closer and closer to us. It was making a sound like that of a grunting hog. Like ferrets peeping over the edge of a dresser drawer, we intently watched the ground below us. Suddenly, there it was! By a child's estimation, it was a monster of enormous proportions, a black bear rooting and snorting at the ground as it went. It stopped right in front of us. Lewis and I were twelve to fifteen feet above this carnivore, and unfortunately, like one of the three little pigs, our fortress was built of straw.

I closed my eyes, for I knew that by now they were so huge that the bear could have seen them in the light of the moon. My stomach knotted up; I felt nauseated and wanted to vomit. Lewis pulled me close to him and kept his hand over my mouth. I knew that he was trying to protect me by keeping me quiet.

The black creature curled up his upper lip and sniffed the air. We could see the long off-white canines glistening in the bright summer night. He moved closer to the bottom of the stacked bales of hay and smelled the ground. After grunting a couple of times, he began to pull at the bales with one of his front paws.

Tears began to well up in my eyes. I wanted to scream, but was unable to make a sound. Fear gripped me so profoundly that I was frozen stiff in my brother's arms. His courage was slipping away as well. I could feel his body starting to tremble. The black bear apparently had no intentions of climbing up to us; he was going to tear down the stacked hay to bring us down to him. We moved away from the front edge of the stacked bales toward the rear of the shed. One by one, the black predator tore down the wall of hay, creating new frontages to the stacked straw as he pawed.

The bear was only moments away from reaching us when we heard the growling and barking of a dog. The yelping became louder and louder and continuous. The creature stopped trying to get to us and turned its attention to the dog that had come up behind it. The dog growled and barked and shifted from side to side. The bear responded with a growl and rushed the dog.

Looking over the edge of the stacked hay at the ensuing battle below us, we watched a brown and white speckled hound dog, the size of a newly born calf, growl and bark and dart from side to side snapping at the bear's flanks. The bear stood up on its hind legs, growled and lunged toward his attacker. Swinging its razor-sharp claws wildly, the bear missed the canine each time by only a whisker. The dog lunged into the bear, took a bite of flesh, and just as quick as lightning jumped clear of the incoming claws. It was as if the dog were nothing more than a set of long white fangs attached to four coiled springs. Not once did the bear seem to make contact.

Finally, the bear grew weary of being under attack. He dropped to his all-fours and started to scamper towards the scrub pine forest that was a couple hundred yards to the north of the shed. The dog stayed right on the bear's heels all the way to the patch of pines. In the darkness we were unable to discern whether one or the other or both went into the dark forest.

As soon as we knew the coast was clear, Lewis and I scrambled down from the top of the stacked bales of hay and ran as fast as our legs could carry us to the screen door of the back porch. For an instant we became wedged in the doorway as we tried to enter at the same time. My brother backed up a step and shoved me through and then came in over top of me. We ran headlong into the kitchen where our mother sat patiently waiting for our return. The table was set with two plates, two glasses of milk, flatware, and all the food that two growing boys could hold.

Lewis was the first to speak. "We're sorry Mom, we're sorry. We will never run away again."

I chimed in, "Me too, Mom, I'm sorry. We will never run away again."

Mom calmly got up from the table and took us into her arms and said, "Well that's good. Are you boys hungry?"

And just like that, we were home. Mom didn't ask us where we had been hiding or anything about our three-hour adventure. She simply asked if we were hungry, and of course we were. When are boys not hungry?

We tried several times to tell her about the bear in our backyard but she would stop us from talking until we had finished our supper. The minute we took our last bites, Lewis and I tried simultaneously to relate how we were being sought after by a huge black bear when this hound dog appeared, fought with the bear, and drove it away. But we were talking so fast and at the same time, Mom finally had to show us her palm and said, "One at a time, please!"

Lewis and I both wanted to tell the story, but I relented, remembering that it was he who had held me close in an attempt to protect me and allay my fears.

My brother started telling Mom how we had not really run away (which did not take her by surprise), how we had come back home keeping the barn between us and the house, how we had hidden on top of the hay in the shed, and how scared we were of the shadows created by blowing grass and leaves and limbs on the trees. Then he described how this black bear had come sniffing around the base of the stacked bails of hay and had begun clawing at the bails to get to us. Then out of nowhere this hound dog had come to our rescue and had driven the bear away.

"You say a dog came to your rescue?" Mom questioned through furrowed brows. "We don't have a dog, so where did the dog come from?"

"We don't know," we responded together.

We had not taken the time to think about the fact that we had no dog. It just appeared out of nowhere and drove the bear away into the thicket of scrub pines behind the house. The dog had simply disappeared after chasing the bear into the woods.

We finally were able to settle down after telling our story, and got ready for bed. It was too late and too dark to go out to look for the mysterious dog or to visit the site of the battle.

The next morning, we arose early and hastened to the rear of the shed. There you could see where several bales of hay had been shredded by the bear's sharp claws. Small pools of blood dotted the ground where the dog had taken several bites out of the bear's hind quarters. However, there was no sign whatsoever of the dog. He had appeared out of nowhere to save us and then had just as quickly vanished. Needless to say, that was the last time Lewis and I faked any kind of running away from home. It was obvious that to obey our mother was a blessing and not a curse.

* * * * * *

There was another "spook" that the Vass family encountered. It happened at Lewis and Betty's home in Shawsville, Virginia. It was the same place where Lewis and I had encountered the copperhead snakes on the top of the hill behind his house. Lewis' two children, Vicki and Tony, were little and had their bedrooms side by side at one end of the house on the lower level. Betty and Lewis had their bedroom on the upper level at the other end of the house.

Practically every night, either Tony or Vicki and sometimes both would end up in bed with their parents. They would declare that something had frightened them out of their sleep.

Tony reported that he would hear a voice speak to him. It was always a woman's voice and she would ask him, "Why are you in my house?"

His sister claimed that she had heard it as well. Sometimes the corner of her room would glow and she insisted that she would see a figure standing there. It was always a hazy outline of a woman dressed in a long flowing white gown.

The children ended up in bed with Lewis and Betty more times than not. They would be shaking all over from being frightened by something. Lewis would grab his flashlight and his service revolver and accompany them to their rooms. He said invariably that he never saw the light or the ghostly figure, nor did he ever hear the voice.

One night, however, only Tony showed up in his parents' bed. Lewis asked him where his sister was and Tony responded that he could hear her through the wall between their rooms talking to someone. Lewis sprang out of bed as if he were the character in the "Night before Christmas." He didn't throw open any sash, but he did grab his 38 caliber revolver and flashlight from the bedside table and ran down the hall to the steps that led to the basement. Betty was right behind him and Tony right behind her. She wanted to check this out as much as Lewis did and Tony wasn't about to be left alone anywhere in that house.

They arrived at Vicki's bedroom and stood just outside her door. Lewis was in the lead holding a flashlight in his left hand and a gun in his right. Betty was holding onto the elastic in her husband's pajama bottoms so tightly that he was getting a wedgie, and Tony was holding on to his mother so tightly and closely that it looked as though Betty and Tony were one person.

The door to Vicki's bedroom was closed, but they could see light coming from underneath the door. In spite of their heavy breathing, they could hear a woman's voice coming from inside.

Lewis turned the doorknob very slowly and quickly pushed the door open. There was Vicki sitting straight up in the middle of her bed starring at a glow in the corner of her room. Just as had been reported, in the midst of the glow one could make out the outline of a woman in a long flowing white gown. She had her arms outstretched, apparently beckoning Vicki to come to her. Lewis and Betty called Vicki's name a couple of times, but she didn't respond. She acted as though she had not even heard them speak to her. My brother finally screamed Vicki's name and she jumped as if she had been shot. When she saw that it was her dad, she flew into his arms crying, "Daddy, Daddy! I'm scared!"

Instantly the figure and the light disappeared. While Betty held Tony and Vicki close to her, Lewis turned on the lamp on the bedside table and searched the room, the closets, the windows, behind the curtains, and under the bed. Nothing! He turned the lights back off and waited a few minutes. Nothing!

The children accompanied their parents to their bedroom and they all slept in one bed that night and many nights thereafter.

After Betty and Lewis saw the light and the figure that night, it never appeared again. Several months later, however, Vicki thought she could hear that same voice making a crying sound somewhere inside the wall at the foot of her bed.

For a while she was too scared to sleep in her own bed. However, as she thought about the situation, it seemed as though the figure was not beckoning to her like she and her Dad had thought, but was somehow reaching out to her. It was as if the figure was upset about something and was seeking comfort. It was impossible to know. The one thing that was certain after that night, Lewis, Betty, nor Tony ever heard the voice or saw the light or the figure again. Vicki, on the other hand, reportedly heard the voice almost every night.

Lewis asked around town if anyone had ever heard of ghostly figures being seen or heard of in that house. Some people at the bank and others at the hardware told him that there had once been a house on the very spot where his house now set. The man that lived there had killed his wife in the basement of the house. He had been discovered, tried, convicted of murder, and executed. The house set empty for a long, long time and eventually had crumbled and just fallen in. Someone had bought the land and removed the remnants of the house and had built the brick home in which Lewis and his family then lived. One of the bank tellers told my brother that the people who had lived in the house before he and Betty, had told her that they heard voices as well, but had never mentioned seeing anything.

After the apparition occurred that night, Vicki said that she never saw anything again. She did hear the voice and the crying, but she was no longer frightened. She would play in her room, sleep there, and hear the sounds, but was no longer scared.

That wasn't true for Tony, however. After that night, if he couldn't sleep with his mom or dad, he kept the door to his room locked and slept in the middle of his bed. I'm sure Tony was glad when they finally moved away from there.

Chapter Seven

A Sick Granny and a Drunken Grandpa; A Mean 'ole Granny and a Quick Tempered Grandpa

Once I saw a commercial on television that literally brought tears to my eyes. It was a Coke commercial where a young married couple with a three year old son had come up to this Victorian style house to visit with the toddler's grandparents. After getting out of their car, the young couple started up the brick-paved walk to the house that had a beautiful wrap-around porch. Bursting through the front screen door, an elderly gray-haired couple came out onto the porch. Laughing with joy at the sight of their son and his family coming to visit, they held their arms straight out as the young couple ran to embrace them.

As soon as he was set free from the car seat, the little boy ran off into the front yard and was instantly greeted by three golden retriever puppies. They knocked the little boy down and smothered him with doggie kisses. The boy rolled back and forth on the ground laughing uncontrollably as the puppies pranced from side to side and licked him all over. It was a precious scene for sure.

Well, that never happened to me. To see the joy of the child being licked all over by the puppies, the smiles on the faces of the grandparents seeing their family coming to visit, and the obvious happiness on the faces of the couple at seeing the grandparents was truly more than I could stand. My eyes would well up with tears at the sight of such joy and happiness between children, grandchildren, and grandparents. I felt ridiculous, but it really touched me. I became emotional over a scene like that because neither set of my grandparents, either on my father's side or my mother's were anything like what the commercial portrayed.

My dad's parents both died in their seventies. Granny (Dad's mom) was bed-ridden for seven years with cancer. I remember she sat up in bed bent forward all those years, constantly moaning from pain. She and her husband (my grandfather) lived with Ralph, their son who had never married. He took care of them until they both passed away.

The last year of her life Granny Vass constantly cried out the name of the son taking care of her. It's a wonder Uncle Ralph didn't lose his mind over having his name called out day and night, but he seemed to let it roll off him like water rolls off a duck's back. Sadly, at the ripe old age of ninety-one Ralph stepped out from between two cars, was struck by an oncoming vehicle, and was killed instantly.

There was something quite interesting about this particular grandmother, however. It seemed that the number seven ran like a thread throughout her life. She had seven sons. She was bed-ridden with cancer for seven years and died at 7:07 on the morning of the seventh day of the week, July 7th, at the age of seventy-seven.

When she died, her back and her buttocks were covered in bed sores from lying in one position for so long. The funeral director told my dad that they had to break her spine in three places in order to be able to lay her out flat. It may sound horrible, but most of the family were relieved (if not happy) when she finally died. Someone who is out of their mind from pain and who is known to be a child of God deserves the right to be out of their misery and be in the presence of their Lord and Savior. At last she was.

Her husband died not too many months later from complications of staying inebriated most of the time. That is how my brother and I remember him, rather messy and drunk.

My grandparents lived in the basement of a mercantile store with Ralph. He owned and ran the store for most of his adult life. The back of their three bedroom flat was underground, but the front was walkout ground level. We went to visit them one Sunday afternoon and as always in my memory, Grandma Elva was in a back bedroom moaning and groaning in pain, constantly calling out her son's name. Whenever he went in to her and asked what she wanted, she never acknowledged his presence, but would continue to rock back and forth and call out, "Ralph, Ralph, Ralph, Ralph...."

Grandpa was sitting in their family room, dozing as a result of his drinking. As always, he was dressed in brown gabardine urine-soiled pants with his suspenders hanging down on either side to his knees. He always wore a pin-striped dress shirt tucked in on one side and hanging out the other, a style that he created many years before its time. The shirt invariably was stained with tobacco juice from dipping snuff. Half inebriated, he would doze off and drool tobacco juice from the corners of his mouth that dropped onto his shirt. Most of the time he would be wearing a pair of untied brown lace-up shoes, with no socks.

When we arrived at their home on this particular Sunday afternoon after church, as usual we found the place in a shambles. Newspapers were scattered about and dirty clothes were lying over the chairs and on top of the stool to the pump organ that sat in the corner of the room. Maxwell House coffee cans with tobacco juice running over the edges sat on the end tables and on the floor beside the chairs. Candy bar wrappers stuck out from underneath the cushions of the sofa, coffee cups and spittoon jars had left circles that marred all the wood surfaces, and black coal dust covered the floor in front of the coal-burning stove that sat about three feet out from the middle of one wall. The once eggshell white walls had turned a dingy gray from years of burning coal for heat. All this was not even visible until the heavy dust-laden maroon damask curtains were pulled back to let some light in for the first time since our last visit.

If it could be possible, the kitchen was even worse. There were scuffed-up base cabinets along the outer wall, which had a sink in the center under a single window. Hanging on either side of the window were wall cabinets with some of the paint chipped off and one of the doors was missing a knob. The base cabinets were streaked down the front from coffee and grease spills. Dirty cups and saucers, plates, and glasses were stacked high in the sink and on the counter tops on either side. There was dried egg yolk on some of the plates and congealed grease on others.

Against the opposite wall set a wooden table and four chairs that were once painted a brilliant white, but were now soiled with black scuff marks, spilled sodas and coffee. There was a faded red and white checkered oilcloth on top of the table. Several strands of the straw lattice work on the bottoms of three of the chairs were frayed and broken. The top of the table was covered with plates and saucers, cups and glasses four and five layers deep. Two of the plates still had partially eaten pork chops, collard greens, and French fries on them from dinner several nights before.

A loaf of Merita bread lay open on a sideboard beside the table. Some of the slices were hard and crusty from hanging out of the bag for a day or two and other slices had signs of being nibbled on by mice. If there were any doubts, rodent droppings were everywhere. On this same sideboard set a thirty-cup coffee maker with dried coffee stains under its spigot and coffee grounds all over the floor in front.

On the wall between the sink and the kitchen table with its four chairs was an electric stove with all four of its burners covered with pots and pans. On one burner set a pot of aging overcooked vegetables that had maggots working to their hearts content, and on another burner set a two-quart pot with four "hard" boiled eggs. The eggs were stuck to the bottom of the pot because all the water had been boiled away. The two remaining burners were occupied by a couple of cast iron pans smeared with charred grease. Since there was no hood over the stove there was a build-up of splattered grease on the wall and on the ceiling. There was not a clean dish or cup, saucer or bowl, pot or pan, or drinking glass in the entire kitchen. Everything was either sitting soiled on top of the stove, on top of the cabinets, on top of the table, or in the sink.

It is hard to imagine, but my Grandpa's bedroom was just as bad. A single cot set against the back wall, a wall that was completely underground. The sheets on the cot were so wrinkled and musty that one could only conclude that they had not been washed in months. A faded green Army blanket that was piled onto the center of the cot reeked of urine. High up on the wall above the cot hung two pictures in matching black oval frames with thick convex glass. The picture on the left was that of an old man with a long white beard. He was wearing round wire-rimmed glasses, a white dress shirt with a stiff collar that was buttoned all the way up, no necktie, and a black wool flannel suit. The other picture was that of an old woman with her salt and pepper hair twisted up tightly into a bun with what looked like two wooden chop sticks pushed through the bun from opposite directions. Her neck was completely covered by a high lace collar atop a plain black dress, and she wore shoes that laced up the front to just above the ankles. Both the man and the woman wore facial expressions that were severe and stern.

On the opposite wall of the room set an old upright mahogany spinet. Its wood was cracked from years of not having oil applied for nourishment, and the color had turned from a brilliant deep red to a dull black. Clothes in need of laundering were piled high on top of the back of the piano. The rest of the long narrow room was filled with cardboard boxes crammed full of old clothes and hundreds of paperbacks as well as hardback books. Some of the books were Zane Gray western novels, some were books on religion, and some were reference books and dictionaries. The room had that "old person smell" about it, musty and earth wormy.

Pieces of paper with writing on both sides were crumpled up and scattered everywhere. Most of the papers where poems and essays written by my grandfather. He had never gone to school, and therefore had no formal education, but he had a passion for learning. He had studied the Webster's Collegiate Dictionary and the World Book Encyclopedias to the point that he could define any word, spell it correctly and use it properly in a sentence. His three given names were John Webster Daniel. He was named after the famous attorney and orator Daniel Webster.

My dad's father may have been an alcoholic, but if he had only been given the opportunity, I just know he could have been someone great. Without any formal training, he could play and tune the banjo, guitar, piano, organ, and violin. He taught individuals how to play these instruments, and he taught group music lessons as well. He was a tinker by trade. As a young man he went around the country tuning people's pianos and organs and stringed instruments. He repaired their sewing machines, vacuums, and ice boxes.

Shortly after our arrival at Grandma's and Grandpa's home, Dad engaged his father in conversation, Lewis and I went off into the back bedrooms to a world of discovery, and Mom spent the entire visit doing laundry, cleaning the house, and cleaning up a kitchen that any health department would most certainly have condemned. On this visit, after mom had finished in the kitchen and moved onto the other parts of the flat, Lewis and I went into the kitchen to explore. That's when we discovered Grandpa's home brew underneath the kitchen sink.

Grandpa had placed some hops, barley, wheat, and yeast in a four gallon earthenware crock filled with water and had covered the whole thing with cheesecloth. Lewis and I carefully peeled back the cheesecloth that covered the crock, skimmed back the layer of scum on top of the liquid, and tasted the concoction brewing in the crock. It didn't take a rocket scientist to detect the smell of alcohol, and the burn that occurred all the way down when it was swallowed let you know that the alcohol content was obviously high.

Even as children we were disgusted at our grandfather for always being thick tongued and disheveled. We thought that it would be funny to teach him a lesson by destroying his alcoholic concoction. We looked through his cabinets and found a five pound bag of salt. We dumped the whole bag into the homebrew beneath the scum and replaced the cheesecloth.

The homemade brew must have been due to be finished within a couple of weeks, for one Sunday afternoon when it was raining and Lewis and I could not go out to play after church, Grandpa called the house. Dad answered the phone and from across the room we could hear Grandpa screaming at him. After hanging up the phone, Dad turned to face us and asked matter-of-factly, "Did you boys pour salt into the crock that was underneath the kitchen sink at Granddad's place?"

Oh how badly we wanted to deny having done so, but honesty was the best policy. I looked down at the floor, but Lewis looked Dad straight in the eyes and answered, "Yes sir, we did."

He stared at us for a few minutes, then said sternly, "You know that you should never bother other people's things, don't you?

We answered together like little robots, "Yes sir!"

In an effort to teach us and have us take part in the solution, Dad asked, "What do you think would be the appropriate punishment?"

There was a moment of silence. Finally Lewis answered with a solemn straight face, "I guess the appropriate punishment would be to not be allowed to visit with Grandpa anymore."

Seeing right through that answer, Dad said, "Oh not so fast, that's not a punishment. I know you boys are never thrilled when we go to visit my parents, and I know that your mother doesn't care for it either, considering she always spends her time there cleaning up awful messes. I understand that they are old and uninteresting to you, but they are my parents and I need to go to see them when I can. They won't be around forever. When they are gone I don't want to regret not having gone to visit them as often as I was able."

Lewis and I looked down at the floor feeling a miniscule sense of remorse. Dad then said to us, "I don't want either of you to ever mess with your grandfather's things again. Do you understand?"

Standing as if we were at attention, we answered, "Yes sir."

"What you did was wrong. I admit however, I would like to have been a fly on the wall to have witnessed him taste that home brew. It must have tasted pretty bad with the salt in it. He shouldn't be making it or drinking it, but at the same time you must never mess with his stuff ever again. Okay?"

Relaxing our posture and putting on a smile to match that of Dad's, we answered, "Okay."

And that was that! After all, how could Dad justify punishing us for destroying what was illegal in the first place?

* * * * * *

There was such a contrast between my dad's parents and my mom's. Dad's mom was frail and sickly. The most she ever weighed in her life, when not pregnant, was a mere ninety-seven pounds. On the other hand my maternal grandmother was a husky woman who worked hard hoeing in the garden until she was elderly. She died at the ripe old age of ninety-two of colon cancer. She might have lived longer, but when she was told several years before her death that she had colon cancer, she refused any treatment, including surgery.

I never witnessed any kind of interaction between my paternal grandmother and grandfather while growing up. She was always in bed sick and he was always "three sheets to the wind." But the interaction between my mom's mother and father was a zebra of different stripes. Most of the time they seemed totally civil to one another; at other times there would be explosions. My grandfather had a violent temper that he kept in check as much as possible.

I remember once Dad had gotten two purebred beagle puppies for Lewis and me. One seemed to be very intelligent while the other seemed to be a little "slow". In any case we had taken the puppies to my grandfather to train to become rabbit dogs. He was known to be the best in the county for training dogs to hunt. He had taken the pups to train and after a couple of weeks we went by to see my grandparents and, of course, our puppies.

After we had been there for a couple of hours, I couldn't stand it any longer. I stood before my grandfather and boldly stated that I wanted to see the puppies. Suddenly, there was frost in the air. Grandpa cut his eyes at Grandma and Grandma cut her eyes at him. Neither one said a word.

Dad was the first to speak. He asked, "Is there something wrong?"

Grandma was the one to respond, "The slower of the two died."

Swallowing like his mouth was full of something, my brother asked, "What do you mean the slower one died?"

Tears welled up in Grandpa's eyes as he attempted to answer, "There was an accident…"

With absolutely no decorum I blurted out, "Accident? What do you mean there was an accident? What kind of accident?"

"Well," Grandpa sighed, "the slower one just didn't seem to catch on to anything. The other puppy would get the point right away, but the slower one….well he just wouldn't get it."

"So what happened to him?" Dad asked matter-of-factly.

With no soft peddling, Grandma blurted out, "Sherm killed him!"

"Grandpa Sherm killed my dog?" I spluttered and began to cry.

With a little more compassion in his voice than Lewis or I would have offered, Dad asked, "What happened?"

I guess my grandfather was too ashamed to answer, so my grandmother did the talking. "One day Sherm had both the pups down in the cleared field where there are several brush piles. Most every one of them had a rabbit or two hiding underneath. Sherm would shake the pile of limbs and when a rabbit came running out from underneath, he put the dogs on it. The 'smarter' one would chase after the rabbit as trained and the other one would just sit there, not making a move. Well, you know Sherm. His temper finally got the best of him. He grabbed the puppy that was "slow" by the skin on his back and slammed him to the ground. The puppy never moved again."

My anger tip-toed away when I watched my grandfather sit there holding his face in his one hand, his broad shoulders shaking as tears dripped steadily from his eyes. In spite of his tremendous temper, his heart was soft and mellow.

My grandmother told us that once he had seen what he had done to the dog, he had broken down in tears and had come to the house where he sat in his recliner the rest of the day, starring off into space. Ever since that terrible day she had seen him with tears in his eyes, eyes that usually glistened with mischief, but now lacked the spark that was normally there.

Everyone knew that Grandpa had a bad temper, but most of the time he was able to keep it under control. He was a strapping hulk of a man, broad in the shoulders and narrow in the hips. He had coal black hair to match his eyes and heavy eyebrows that formed a canopy overtop. He invariably wore long sleeved flannel plaid shirts and blue denim bibbed overalls. The right sleeve of his shirt was always rolled up and pinned halfway between his shoulder and where the elbow would have been. His right arm had been amputated up to that level.

When he was a young man harvesting trees for lumber out of the sides of the mountains in southwest Virginia, a mule that had been dragging logs decided to sit down and rest. Grandpa pulled on the mule's reigns, pushed on his rump, kicked, prodded, yelled, and screamed, all to no avail. He got so angry that he finally lost control. He balled up his right hand into a fist and hit the sterile hybrid square between the eyes, knocking the animal unconscious. The skin on his knuckles was not only bruised, but split. It must have hurt like crazy, but he continued to work the mountainside the rest of the day. By the time he got home that evening the split in his hand had become infected.

This was several years before the advent of the first antibiotic, penicillin in 1948. When my grandfather got home, my grandmother cleaned his wound and poured horse liniment over it as she did for everything in those days, but the infection continued to worsen. The infection finally began spreading as red streaks up his arm above his wrist. The local doctor knew that he would be unable to stop the infection, so he sent my grandfather to the nearest hospital for treatment. The nearest hospital was over a couple of hours away.

Unfortunately, without antibiotics the doctors at the hospital could not stop the spread of the infection up my grandfather's arm. They had to amputate his hand above the infected area. The amputation, however, was not far enough up the arm. Infection continued in the surgical site until it had reached the elbow of his right arm. This time the surgeon amputated the arm far above the infected site, midway between the elbow and the shoulder. After that, Grandpa had no more infection in that limb and it finally healed over.

The strange thing about that amputated arm, however, was the fact that Grandpa could sometimes feel pain in the hand that was no longer there. It's called phantom pain and many amputees experience it.

Amazingly, even with only one arm, Grandpa could lift more with his left hand and arm than most men could lift using both their limbs. One time a trailer loaded with cut logs was being pulled out of the mountain side by a team of horses and the trailer turned over. The logs spilled off the side of the trailer and rolled down the side of the mountain into an area that could only be reached on foot. The men that had been walking along side of the trailer guiding the horses by their reigns went down into the ravine to recover the runaway logs. Together they could not manage them. However, my grandfather went down to where they were, and with his one good arm picked up the logs, one at a time, and carried them out unaided. Like I said, he was a strong hulk of a man.

It is interesting to note that Grandpa always wore dress shoes and work boots that laced up. With the one remaining hand he somehow was able to tie his own shoes, load tobacco into his own pipe, and light it himself. On one Christmas Sunday morning (when I was sixteen years old) Grandpa was sitting in his favorite recliner. He bent over to tie his shoes, but he never rose up again. He died of cardiac arrest while lacing up his dress shoes, getting ready for church.

Grandma Sherm (her name was Levada, but everyone called her Grandma Sherm and her husband Grandpa Sherm) never forgave my grandfather for dying first. She had always prepared for it, planned for it, and never dreamed that she would not be the first to go. When Grandpa Sherm died first, it not only took her by surprise, it infuriated her. She had attempted to be the first to die once before.

Many years prior to Grandpa's Christmas morning death, before I was even born, Grandma had decided that she was going to die. She had had a cold for a protracted period of time and had come to the conclusion that this was her time to go. Since she thought that Grandpa could not make it without her, she had made provisions to sell their farm. They did indeed sell their farm and Grandma was bed ridden for some length of time. But when she got better and realized that her impending death was a false alarm, they had to start over. Grandpa searched around and found a nearby farm for sell. He purchased that farm and life began again.

Grandma was extremely hard of hearing. She wore a hearing aid in each ear, the old fashioned type, which had a battery pack the size of a pack of cigarettes that she kept stuffed down inside the front of her bra between her breasts. From this battery pack ran twisted flesh-colored rubber coated wire to each hearing aid receiver in each ear. She kept the wires tucked up underneath her ringlet-curled gray hair. Like so many old women she kept her hair dyed a silver-blue. Because of her extremely poor hearing and in spite of wearing double hearing aids, Grandma apparently hated when a television was on because she could not hear it or understand what the people were saying. Because she could not enjoy what was on the television, she refused to allow Grandpa Sherm to enjoy it either. In their entire lives they never owned a television set.

On the few occasions when they ever came to my mom and dad's home to visit, Grandma would always manage to sabotage Grandpa's TV viewing. She would either manage to station herself in front of the TV console or talk so loudly when the program was on that no one could hear and enjoy it.

Having to start your life over might be a struggle for some, but Grandma was a savvy business woman. She was one of the first female business owners I ever knew. She was a chicken rancher. She had all the machinery, buildings, fixtures, incubators, and five thousand chickens.

Most of the chickens were being raised for market, but I remember that she had a number of fowl that she kept for the production of eggs.

Sometimes when we would be at her home visiting, she would hand me a basket and instruct me to go into the chicken yard, into the building where the chickens roosted at night, and gather the eggs.

I was frightened of these smelly feathered creatures, but Grandma Sherm would send Lewis or me (or both) anyway to gather her eggs with instructions not to bother the hens if they were sitting on their nests. We were simply to push our hand gently underneath the chicken and remove the eggs without causing them to leave their post. Many times they would attempt to peck our hands. When this happened, I was not about to let some orange-feathered, bill-pecking, red-eyed, biped put a mark on me, especially when I was sent to gather the eggs alone. I would approach the nest and with an open palm slap the chicken across her face. This would send the bird flying across the room. Then I could gather the eggs unimpeded. I am relatively sure that I never told my grandmother about how I had solved the pecking problem.

Even though the chicken house and the chicken yard were surrounded by a ten foot high chicken-wire fence, they would occasionally get out. After all, chickens can fly for short distances. There was always a hen or two wandering around my grandmother's yard. Grandma was a flower-growing fanatic. Every inch of available space on her front and back porches was taken up with ceramic pots or coffee cans filled with flowers. On either side of the front steps, the back steps, and around every tree in the yard she had planted beds of flowers. Chickens love to scratch in the dirt around flowers to dig up worms to eat. To prevent this, my grandmother had strung electric wire low to the ground between the rows of flowers. The majority of the time the chickens would feel the electricity in the air and shy away from the flower beds. Sometimes they were not so intuitive, and would be found dead, stuck to the wire by their bills.

There was an occasion when my Grandmother hosted a party for a bunch of women at her house. It was what they used to call a "Hen party." Neither she nor my grandfather consumed alcoholic beverages, but she always served a marvelous strawberry punch. Their house had only one bathroom and Grandpa had enjoyed the strawberry punch just as much as the ladies had. It was nearing nine o'clock and the one and only bathroom had been continually tied up all evening. Grandpa was about to burst. He decided to take advantage of the total darkness of the back porch. He went off alone into the darkness to relieve himself over the railing of the back porch. A blood curdling scream came from the rear of the house. Everyone there and within a five-mile radius heard the shrill scream. Everyone stopped to listen, but no further screams or sounds were heard. Everyone eventually returned to doing what they had been doing before hearing the terrible screech.

The next morning when Grandma went out to water her flowers, she found that every last one of them by the back porch had been stomped into the ground. She remembered the scream and decided it best not to say anything to Grandpa about her flowers being trampled under foot. A short time later she decided that she didn't need that electric wire. After all, two or three chickens were being electrocuted every month or so and that seemed a tad too many.

After Grandpa had died on that Christmas morning and was laid to rest on top of the hill where my mother's family cemetery was, Grandma Sherm decided to sell their house and farm and move in with us. Before she did, however, we had a basement dug beside our house that tied into the existing basement and erected on top of this a twenty by forty foot room. It was divided into a kitchen, a bathroom, and a living room/bedroom combination. Grandma moved in shortly after the construction had been completed. It seemed to go well. She had her own private quarters, and at the same time had people just on the other side of a door that could respond to her as needed.

On most nights after she had prepared her own dinner and washed her dishes, she would join us in our family room. She would not want anyone to ever know it, but after some interactive conversation, after things had settled down and we were watching a TV program, we observed her watching and enjoying something that she would never have let her husband ever enjoy. What a shame!

She must have lived there in the adjoining apartment for three or four years. On one occasion I was getting ready to go to the barn to milk the cows when I heard a dreadful moaning sound coming from Grandma's apartment. None of us would ever go into her place without knocking first, but the sound was so disturbing that I burst in without knocking. There was Grandma standing in front of the kitchen sink washing dishes. She was making that dreadful noise that I had heard, and evidently had her hearing aids turned off. I stood very quietly for a moment or two and listened to the words. I realized that she was singing *Amazing Grace*. The tune was anything but *Amazing Grace*, but the words were unmistakable. That's when I came to the conclusion that she couldn't carry a tune in a bushel basket. Realizing that there was no emergency, except the need for singing lessons, I backed out slowly and closed her door. Smiling like a Cheshire cat, I went on to take care of my chores, singing *Amazing Grace* to myself.

I always felt that my mother's mother must be one of the meanest women I had ever known. Anyone who was unkind to animals had to have a mean streak. I observed Grandma doing some pretty strange things when it came to animals. One day I happened to be looking out the window that faced onto the porch in front of my grandmother's apartment and watched her entice a small stray cat to come to her. In our barn lived several very wild cats, so wild in fact that they normally couldn't be touched or petted. No one had invited them to live there, but cats appear as if by spontaneous generation when there are mice about. I didn't recognize this young feline that my grandmother was inviting onto her porch. She had placed a lid from a gallon mayonnaise jar filled with milk on the edge of the porch. Bent over at the waist, she was calling, "Kitty, kitty, come here kitty, kitty."

Finally the nervous kitten came onto the edge of the porch and began to lap up the milk that was in the jar lid. Once the young feline was preoccupied with consuming the milk, my grandmother slowly reached around behind her and produced a broom. She began to thrash the kitten across the back with the broom like a farmer striking a bundle of wheat against the floor of a granary. She made horrible screeching noises that if I had not been privy to the source of the sound, I wound have been scared as well. She only hit the cat with the straw at the end of the broom which would not have caused any injury, but the thought of tormenting an animal for no good reason certainly in my mind qualified my Grandmother as one of the meanest women I had ever known.

After some three and a half years, Grandma finally came to the conclusion that she would rather live next to her son than next to her daughter. She communicated this very clearly in her mean old woman manner to my mother. Mom was beside herself. She wanted to know what she had done to her mother to cause her to want to move away. Dad finally was able to convince her that it was nothing she had done; it was simply Grandma's way. She apparently just liked her son better than she had ever liked any of her three daughters. I'm sure my Uncle Rex brought up the subject of her living near him every time he came to visit her.

Uncle Rex lived only about four miles away and you could see that he didn't like the fact that Grandma had chosen to live with one of her daughters and not with him. I believe he ultimately convinced her to buy a house trailer and park it in the field next to his yard. That is what she did.

I know it hurt my mother's feelings, but it was certainly not a bad move for the rest of us. Having the extra room in that wing of the house made available to us was certainly a blessing. Besides, my brother married at age sixteen. He and his new bride made the basement of that wing their new home for two years until he and Betty finished high school. After they graduated, they bought a new house trailer, parked it next to the highway on their own lot, and moved out of the basement.

That is when it became <u>my</u> new haven. How wonderful it was. I could stay up late on weekend nights watching "Dark Shadows" and "77 Sunset Strip" with Kookie Burns, Connie Stevens, and Efrin Zimbelist, Jr. Ah, that was the teenage life back then!

After Grandma moved out, we would go out to visit her in her new trailer. It had that new trailer burn-your-eyes formaldehyde smell for a long time. There did come a time when you stopped noticing it. Mom always stopped by the grocery store and took Grandma her staple foods. She would fill a couple of shopping bags with frozen beef and pork from our freezer, fresh vegetables from our garden in summer, home canned vegetables, sausage, and preserves in winter, and take them to Granny as well.

I never was brave enough to visit my grandmother alone. I needed someone to translate for me. For some reason she never understood a word I said. Mom or Lewis or Dad or someone else present would have to repeat my every word before Grandma understood what I had said. There was just something about my voice that prevented her from understanding me. It was quite frustrating and annoying.

Whenever we went to see Grandma Sherm, she would always be sitting in the same spot, in a brown naugahide platform rocker with her feet propped up on a padded stool. She had made her own footstool from an oak bar stool she had bought at Woolworth's. To make it the right height, she had shortened the legs with a handsaw and capped their ends with rubber caps like those found on the end of canes. On the top of the wooden stool she had placed a four-inch thick piece of foam rubber and covered it with red satin material that she had smocked all around. With her feet up, she sat in that rocker facing the screen door that opened onto her front porch. That way she could observe the traffic going by and watch for anyone that might come to see her. I always felt that it was so she could be prepared to swat visitors with her broom.

Granny suffered with arthritis, the type that had twisted the digits of both her hands and her feet. The disease had twisted her toes so severely that large corns had developed on the tops of the joints wherever her toes rubbed against the inside of her shoes. She wore black leather "old lady" shoes. After buying a new pair, she would take a razor blade and cut out holes in the tops of the shoes over the callused joints to relieve the pressure.

Like her toes, Grandma's fingers were so twisted and turned from arthritis that whenever she pointed at something, you were never sure what the object of her intention actually was.

Once when Mom and I had gone to visit Grandma Sherm in her new trailer, taking her bags full of food, we were not there very long when out of the blue Grandma said, "I tell you what's the truth, if I had known what a heartache it would be to have children, I would never have had them."

You could have knocked my mother over with a feather. Her mouth literally dropped open. Big tears welled up in her eyes and she asked, "Why in the world would you say such a thing, Mom?"

"Because it's true," she responded curtly. "Children are nothing but heartaches."

I really felt for Mom. She had come to visit her own mother, had brought her a bounty of groceries, and just like that, Grandma hit her over the head with her "straw broom of words". Grandma had given birth to two sons, one of whom died a few days after birth. She also brought four daughters into the world, one of whom also died quite young. None of her children had ever been in any kind of trouble. They all had made good livings. None of her grandchildren had ever been in trouble. All her children and their children had been quite successful and productive. Why in the world my grandmother would have said something so mean and cruel to a daughter who had shown her nothing but love? Only God knew. Could it have been pure unadulterated meanness? I guess we'll never really know.

There were other occasions when my grandmother would clobber you with her broom of words. When we were teenagers, my mother talked my brother and me into going to visit our grandmother. She said that it would mean so much to her mother if we would just show up for a visit by ourselves. We reluctantly agreed. It was only out of our deep respect and love for our sweet mother that we went.

We thought about changing our clothes for the visit, but decided since it was mid-August shorts and overhanging t-shirts should be alright. Lewis did most of the talking (as usual), "translating" for Grandma the things that I had said.

We stayed with her for about an hour. She had been pleasant enough. Then out of the blue she pointed her crooked index finger in our direction and matter-of-factly said, "I tell you what's the truth, there's nothing sorrier than a boy or man that won't tuck his shirt tail in."

We sat there stunned! Just like that kitten drinking milk out of a mayonnaise jar lid on Grandma's front porch, she had flogged us with her broom.

Lewis looked at his watch and said, "Well! Where has the time gone? We've got to go, Granny."

We got to our feet and walked to the door in front of her platform rocker and without any further ado, said our goodbyes. She told us as we left that she had enjoyed our visit, and asked us to come back as often as we could.

Right! Like that was going to happen!

After I had finished college and dental school and my wife had entered the teaching field, we dropped by Granny's trailer to pay her our respects. We were hoping that she was not home, but no such luck. She still couldn't understand the words that I spoke. She could understand my wife, however, so she did most of the talking, "translating" for me.

My wife told my grandmother all about her experiences as a chemistry teacher. Granny didn't even know what chemistry was and there was no point in trying to explain it. I had no idea why I was surprised, but without warning, Granny pointed her crooked finger in the direction of my wife and said, "I tell you what's the truth, there's nothing sorrier than a school teacher."

She went right back to looking at her fingertips as she touched them together like a spider doing pushups on a mirror. This was a habit she had when she had said what she wanted to say, and there was nothing else to add.

My wife huffed, "Well, I never!"

I reached over and placed my hand on hers, looked into her eyes, and shook my head slightly from side to side. After all, what was the use of raising a fuss? Granny was Granny and there was no changing her. Needless to say, it was now time to go.

There was something that my grandmother would invariably say almost every time I was in her presence. Conversations would always drift to someone that my grandmother thought very little of, whether they were just plain "sorry," or whether she considered them crooked or perverse, or whether she simply didn't like them. Pointing her twisted arthritic finger somewhere in my direction, she would say in her flat drawn-out mountain dialect, "I tell you what's the truth,

Larry**; hell's too good for some people!**" She would then return to staring at her fingertips doing spider pushups on a mirror.

I suppose when a person's mind always dwells on the negative aspects of life, they are incapable of taking pleasure in members of their family or anyone else for that matter. If they remain angry over their spouse having the audacity to die first, if they display cruelty to animals (including the Homo sapiens variety) as if that were "normal," they would certainly believe that "**hell's too good for some people**."

Chapter Eight

Too Much Dynamite and a Lot of Bull

Growing up on a farm in the fifties and early sixties certainly encompassed many interesting and challenging moments. Recalling some of the more "explosive" moments can be funny in retrospect.

In those mid-twentieth century decades and before, anyone could go to any local mercantile store and buy a medicine called *Paregoric*. *Paregoric* was a liquid that, when mixed with sugar and warm water, would settle any sick or upset stomach. It could also be rubbed on gums to relieve a toothache. There should be no doubt about its efficacy; *Paregoric* was pure opium.

As a pre-teen, I spent many Saturdays with my Uncle Ralph. He ran a business that was a combination of grocery store, gas station, deli, and clothing store. Many times when I was there visiting with

Uncle Ralph, an old man named Albert Witherspoon would come into my uncle's store and buy a Stanback or B.C. Power (aspirin) and a Coca-Cola. He would open the packet of powder, pour the contents into his mouth, and wash it down with the entire bottle of Coke. For a total of twenty cents he could have that "good feeling" all day long. In the "fifties" when the soft drink Coca-Cola was mixed with powdered aspirin, it gave the person drinking it quite a "buzz." Coke, after all, got its name from the fact that the original formula possessed a hint of cocaine.

Anyone needing explosives in those days could go to the local hardware store and, with the stroke of a pen, buy sticks of dynamite along with the fuses and caps necessary to set them off. You didn't have to be in construction, just a sober adult. One might be a farmer in need of removing a stump after a tree had been cut down or splitting a large boulder into pieces that could be handled. Dad always kept a case of dynamite stored away in the back of the "white building" for a variety of uses on the farm.

One of those explosive opportunities came when a number of locust trees had been cut down in the field in front of the house. Normally when trees were removed from our farm, they would be taken away to the mill and turned into lumber. Either Dad or whoever had purchased the trees from him got the sawed wood. However, locust was not a wood good enough to be used as dressed boards to make furniture, frame a house, or to be made into cabinets or bookcases. Basically, locust wood was only good to burn in a fireplace or to make fence posts. However, if one burned locust wood for heat in a fireplace, the chimney had to be cleaned more than once a year. The risk of chimney fires was great because of the rapid buildup of creosote.

There remained probably ten stumps after the locust trees had been cut down and carried away. Our Ford farm tractor was not powerful enough to pull any of the stumps out of the ground. Dynamite! That was the solution. Most everyone knew (that is, anyone who had any dealings with dynamite) that a quarter stick of dynamite was usually enough explosive to take a tree stump out of the ground. Dad, however, always felt that if a quarter stick would do the task, a whole stick would work wonders.

One of the locust stumps designated for removal was on the edge of a gully about a football field's length from the house. The wedge-shaped gully was about three feet deep and was created by water that had rushed from the top of the hill after several rain storms. At Dad's direction, Lewis got down into the gully and dug a hole deep enough to place some explosives underneath the exposed roots of the stump. Once Lewis stepped back from his digging, Dad moved in to do his part. After fastening a blasting cap onto a ten inch fuse, he pushed the fuse and blasting cap into the semi-soft stick of dynamite and placed it into the hole underneath the stump. He carefully covered the stick with dirt, removed his lighter from his shirt pocket, lit the fuse, and quickly scrambled out of the ditch. He yelled, "Run boys! Get behind the tractor."

When the dynamite went off, the explosion was so loud it caused us to experience temporary deafness. With our ears still ringing we looked out over the hood of the Ford tractor, but there was no stump, just a large hole in the ground with smoke bellowing up. The amount of dynamite Dad used was enough to send the entire locust stump so high into the sky that we could not see it. Realizing this to be the case, Dad instructed us to crawl underneath the tractor until the stump returned to earth.

Peering out from underneath the belly of the tractor, we could finally see a tiny speck in the sky. We watched it for a few moments and then Dad yelled, "Here she comes!"

Like the whistling sound of a bomb accelerating toward earth, the stump hit the ground no less than three yards from the tractor, kicking up a cloud of dirt and dust ten feet high. Within seconds after the impact, root fragments and dirt rained down like hail pelting the earth during a bad storm.

The explosion produced such strong shock waves that the canned goods on the shelves of the country store a quarter mile away came crashing to the floor. The door to the Franklin wood burning stove in one end of the store flew open and the old men that usually sat around on empty nail kegs playing checkers and other board games took cover underneath the booths and countertops. The windows at the store and at our house rattled. A few panes cracked. Our kitchen cabinet doors flew open, but amazingly, no dinnerware or glassware was damaged.

Mom had not been warned about the impending explosion. She knew instinctively, however, that this had to be Dad's doing. She came running out of the house yelling his name.

The look on Dad's face was priceless. In an instant he knew that he should have warned Mom about what was coming. The look said, 'Oh brother, I'll never hear the end of this.'

Lewis and I were of no help. We both added, "Oh Mom, you should have seen it. Why that stump went plum out of sight. We had to crawl under the tractor so it wouldn't hit us. And when it finally came back down, it must have rained dirt and roots for at least five minutes."

"That's enough, boys," Dad said sheepishly. "It didn't rain those things for five minutes."

"It doesn't matter," Mom said tersely. "The fact is, you used too much dynamite and you put not only yourself in danger but the boys as well."

"We were never in any danger," Dad replied as he took a step backwards.

"Are you kidding?" Mom snapped. "Every time you three go out of the house, there's danger, either to yourselves, to each other, or to someone else! I swear, if you don't kill each other first, you'll be the death of me."

After a severe tongue lashing, Dad promised to do better next time.

She whirled around and headed back to the house. Dad knew that he had been in the wrong. We watched her through our eyebrows. Once she entered the back door of the house, Dad turned to us and said with a grin, "Okay boys, let's get this mess cleaned up."

He might have been in the doghouse with Mom, but clearly he enjoyed the rush of the event.

It wasn't long after we cleared the field of all the stumps and smoothed out the dirt with a grader blade on the back of the tractor, that Dad decided that we needed a full basement under the house. He wanted to replace the coal burning Franklin stove in the den with a central oil burning furnace. To bring that to fruition, we needed a basement.

We began digging about ten feet from the foundation of the house and dug a dirt ramp into the ground underneath the double windows of the living room. I don't remember Dad ever actually wielding a mattock or a shovel, but he could certainly give good instructions. He was a born supervisor. After about a week of digging, we had achieved a dirt ramp to the depth of about seven feet. Once Dad installed a metal lentil, we started going straight in underneath the foundation of the house. When we were about four feet in, we hit solid granite. At this point we started drilling holes into the granite to set explosives to split the rock. It never occurred to me to caution Dad, who was the only one allowed to handle the explosives. Thus, because the stump episode had completely escaped his memory, Dad placed a full stick of dynamite into the hole and tamped it in until it was no longer exposed. On top of this he packed some mud and lit the fuse. We ran out from under the house, raced up the ramp, and scampered out into the yard well away from the entrance to the dig.

"Caboom!" Dirt, rock fragments, smoke, and the shovel we had left behind on the dirt floor all came flying like missiles out from underneath the house. The panes of the double windows directly over the dig rattled, shook, cracked and fell out. Some of the white asbestos shingles cracked and pieces fell off exposing the black weatherproof paper underneath. All the doors on the kitchen cabinets flew open. Plates and glasses and saucers crashed onto the floor. Pots and pans hit the floor from the base cabinets. The oven door dropped down and the pressure relief valve on the lid of a pressure cooker being heated on top of the stove lodged in place. The pressure inside the cooker began to build and a moment later, the lid to the pressure cooker blew. Straight up it went. The valve stem with its lid stuck into the kitchen ceiling, pinto beans, and their thick juice covered everything. Canisters fell off the countertop onto the floor, intermingling their contents of sugar, white flour, salt, and brown sugar. It was a huge mess!

Lewis and I were jumping up and down, dancing around like natives doing a war dance when Mom came charging out the back door. We heard the screen door slam hard. Immediately we stopped our cavorting. The look on her face was not good. We felt safe enough from her wrath, but Dad was a different story. She came running up to Dad as if she would continue right on through him.

"Are you crazy?" Mom screamed into his face. "I thought for sure after you blew that stump to kingdom-come you would have sense enough to know that you don't use a sledge hammer to kill a flea. How much dynamite did you use anyway? How much?"

Mom stood there with her arms crossed glaring into Dad's eyes. She was tapping her foot on the ground so fast it reminded me of a happy dog wagging its tail. But happy she was not. Repeating herself, she said, "How much?"

Dad dropped his head like a little boy caught in the act of doing something he shouldn't have been and answered, "Just one stick, Dear. I only used one stick."

"Why in the world so much, Carbin?" she asked with disgust in her voice. "Why did you use an entire stick of dynamite under our home?"

Dad started to stutter as he did when he was nervous, "Well… well…well, I…I…I thought that because we were trying to split sol… sol…solid rock, that it would take that much."

Mom just shook her head. "Did it ever occur to you," she asked, "that you try a little piece first and if that doesn't split the rock, then you can go bigger? You don't start with the largest piece first and hope for the best. Your dinner is all over the kitchen floor and ceiling and cabinets. Some of my dishes and glasses are broken, and we will have to buy all new sugar and flour and salt and brown sugar. They are mixed together all over the kitchen floor. Just look at the side of the house and the broken window panes; they'll have to be replaced as well. Money doesn't grow on trees you know, unless you've discovered some money tree in our back yard…." She trailed off as she started to cry.

That was all it took. No one wanted to see Mom cry, especially Dad. He followed her into the house through the back screen door repeating over and over, "I'm sorry. I'm sorry."

That was it for the day. No more digging and no more explosions. For the rest of this day anyway, there needed to be total silence. Lewis and I went around to the back of the house to the "white building."

There we could make something to play with until another day of digging began.

It was a week before we resumed our project underneath the house, not because Mom had been so upset at the dynamite going off under her feet, but it had rained for a couple of days. The dirt ramp had carried the rainwater into the excavated area so that there was two to three inches of standing muddy water, and the ramp itself had turned into a red clay slide.

Once the rains ceased, Dad rented a sump pump to drain the water from the dig. He called for a truck load of blue shell gravel from the rock quarry near Pulaski, Virginia to be delivered to our house. Lewis and I shoveled the load of gravel onto the mud floor.

The week of no digging was also spent replacing the broken window panes and broken shingles. The lid of Mom's pressure cooker was removed from the ceiling, and a fresh coat of paint was applied to the kitchen ceiling and walls. Dad had to promise to significantly reduce the amount of dynamite used and to send either Lewis or me to announce when the charge would be set off. That way Mom could tape the cabinet doors shut and move things down from the countertops to the floor. Since Dad's explosions were perceived all over the immediate area as a restart of WW II or a notable shift in the plutonic plates, he also had promised to notify the people living in the area of his impending use of explosives as well.

Digging the basement beneath our house took almost three months. We opened a hole in the ground beside the back porch and, using cinderblock, built steps that came from our newly dug basement to the back door of the kitchen. A truck load of concrete was delivered by a local cement company and poured onto the gravel-covered dirt floor by way of a wooden sluice that was placed on the ramp used to haul out the dirt from the dig. Dad hired an out-of-work brick mason to shore up the walls with cinderblock.

Lewis and I used the rear blade on the farm tractor to backfill the ramp. After we leveled and hared the dirt, we scattered tall fescue grass seed and covered it with straw. The basement had become a reality, and Mom's dishes were once again safe, at least for the moment.

"An acorn does not fall far from the tree." Everyone has at one time or another heard this truism. You might say that the use of powder ran in our veins. Every Christmas, Dad would purchase firecrackers, Roman candles, cherry bombs, and M-80's from Uncle Ralph, who never revealed the source of his fireworks. It didn't matter to Lewis or me anyway. We always looked forward to having these treasured items to play with for a month or two after Christmas.

I've had a few firecrackers explode in my hands over the years. The skin on my fingers would scorch black from the powder and they would sting for a few minutes, but thankfully no serious injuries ever resulted. Fortunately, no cherry bombs or M-80's ever exploded in our hands. That would have been a different matter. Those things could take off a finger or two if they were to go off while holding them, which would certainly have prevented me from ever becoming a dentist and Lewis from having a successful career as a state policeman.

After changing the oil in the farm tractor and the cars we threw the empty aluminum oil cans that remained into an enclosed bin behind the "white building". They were kept there until the bin filled up. Once that happened, we bagged them up and carried the load off to the county landfill.

Just another illustration of how God protected us against ourselves and one another, Lewis and I would light either cherry bombs or M-80's, drop them down through the punctured hole in top of the aluminum oil cans and throw them at each other. When our "grenades" exploded, pieces of metal went everywhere. If any of the leftover oil in the can got on either one of us, it was considered a hit. The person being soiled with oil was considered a casualty of the conflict. Not once did a piece of shrapnel ever hit our exposed skin, or ever put out one of our eyes or cut a gash into our faces or hands. That had to have been a pure miracle wrought of God. He was saving us for better things.

Speaking of God, the first time that I ever actually remember falling to my knees and praying for His intervention in a situation or begging for a miracle was over a blast of a cherry bomb. Our milk cow, affectionately known as "'Ole Mousey" played the major role in my first need of Divine intervention. She was standing all alone in the barnyard licking a salt block. I came up to her and like always she did not move away, but continued with what she was doing. I don't remember what I was thinking at the time, or if indeed I was thinking at all, but I took a cherry bomb from the left side pocket of my jacket and lit it. I placed it on the crown of 'Ole Mousey's head and stepped back to see what would happen when the miniature explosive went off.

The cherry bomb fizzled for a second or two and then "caboom!" The sound of the cherry bomb could probably have been heard for a country mile. 'Ole Mousey's eyes rolled so far back into her head that the whites of her eyes were all that could be seen. She reeled from side to side, not unlike the time she was drunk from eating dried leaves on a downed cherry tree. Her legs buckled and that bovine hit the ground like that rocketed stump plummeting from above.

I ran over to the downed cow and pushed on her side to no avail. She wouldn't move. I pulled her upper eyelids open wide–nothing but white. I dropped to my knees so fast that I didn't even notice until later that my right knee had come down on a rock. I started to pray, "My God and my Father, oh please, oh please, oh please, don't let 'Ole Mousey die."

I opened one eye and looked over at 'Ole Mousey. The hair on the crown of her head between the stumps where her horns had been removed years before was smoldering. There was a bald spot about the size of a baseball where the hair had been completely blown away. The edges around this area were blackened by the scorched powder.

"Please, please, please, Oh God," I repeated quickly, as if speed was of the essence. "Revive 'Ole Mousey. Please don't let her die. I'll never do something so foolish again. I promise. I'll obey Mom, and Dad, and I'll even do what my brother tells me to do. Please don't let 'Ole Mousey die!"

Finally she started to move. Her tongue was hanging out of the corner of her mouth, and a white froth was bubbling up as if she had hydrophobia. She started to bawl like a calf hungry for her mother's milk. She struggled to get to her feet and stood there swaying from side to side. The pupils of her eyes had not yet reappeared.

'Oh my God,' I thought, 'I've blown the black centers of her eyes off! Dad will know for sure what I have done. Please, Oh Lord, can't you just paint the black centers back on her eyes?'

I closed my eyes and squeezed them so tightly together they almost hurt. I prayed like I had never prayed before. "Oh Lord," I said, "If you could only restore this old cow, I'll do anything. I won't complain about going to church anymore. I will be a model son."

"No problem," said a voice that was deep and gruff. "I'll save the cow, but you have got to turn over a new leaf."

"I will, I will," I mumbled. "I'll do anything. This is our best cow, Lord. She gives four gallons of milk at each milking. But you know that, don't you?"

"Know what?" the voice asked.

Suddenly the Almighty's voice didn't sound so sure! Whether I muttered something out loud or under my breath, wouldn't He know what I said regardless? I opened my eyes and saw my brother standing in front of me smiling.

I started screaming at my brother, "You jerk, you total jerk! Why are you messing with me?"

As I hurled curses, I swung my fists at him wildly. Unfortunately I missed the mark every time. Lewis ducked and dodged, laughing at me all the while.

He finally stopped his bobbing and weaving and put the palm of his hand on my forehead. "That's enough," he said, "You did what you did to 'Ole Mousey, not me. What did you do to her anyway?"

"Oh. I just put off a cherry bomb on top of her head, that's all," I answered both smugly and a bit timidly.

Lewis doubled over with laughter. He couldn't contain himself. He tried to speak, but his words came out in spurts. "You set...set off...off a cherry bomb on her head. Hee haw! Hee hee!" he went on and on.

"Yeah, that's right. I set off a cherry bomb on 'Ole Mousey's head and she went down like she'd been shot. It scared me half to death," I cried.

"I can imagine," my big brother commented in derision. He walked over to where 'Ole Mousey stood swaying back and forth and brushed the smoke out of her hair with his hand. "Well, she's standing now. That's a lot better than when I first came upon you two."

As if this was the most important thing in my life, I asked my big brother, "Does she have any color in her eyes?"

"Why do you want to know if she has any color in her eyes?" my brother queried.

Half crying, I answered, "Because I think the cherry bomb blew the black dots off her eyes. They disappeared when she went down."

Lewis began to howl with laughter all over again.

I screamed at him, "Don't laugh at me! This is serious!"

"Okay, Okay," he said. "Let's see if her eyes are alright now."

He went over to 'Ole Mousey and raised the lids of her eyes. "See!" he pointed out, "the black dots have returned. They simply disappeared when she fell unconscious. Her eyes are starting to return to normal."

"Thank you Jesus," I squealed with glee. "Thank you for saving 'Ole Mousey and her black dots."

"I don't think that the cherry bomb would have killed her," my brother added, "but I'm not so sure she will ever be able to hear us call her again. We need to tell Dad about this."

I grabbed Lewis' arm like one begging for his life and pleaded, "No, no, we can't tell Dad! He will kill me! Please don't tell Dad!"

Being very coy, my brother pulled on his chin as if in deep thought. Finally he said, "Well, I'm not so sure that is a good idea. What if something is different about 'Ole Mousey now? We might need to clear the air with Dad."

I was too young to realize then that I was being had. Lewis had no intentions of telling Dad anything. He just wanted control over my life. He needed me to be indebted to him.

I pleaded all the more, "Oh please, Lewis, don't tell Dad what I did. He will be so mad at me!"

"Well, that's true," Lewis said as he watched me out of the corner of his eye. "Dad would be very upset and probably would have to disown you for what you have done. I <u>am</u> the older brother, but to see you sent away, well, I love you too much to ever have that happen."

I didn't realize that he was playing me like a fiddle. I was frightened half to death. I needed him to keep silent and not to tell Mom or Dad the heinous thing that I had done.

Lewis finally said to me, "I tell you what, Larry, I will keep silent about what you have done, but I own you, do you understand? You have to do whatever I say!"

"Anything, I will do anything!" I said. "Anything!"

"Okay," my big brother said cheerfully. "As long as we understand each other."

"Oh, we do, we do," I added without hesitation, "no problem here, whatever you say."

I should have recognized the demonic smile that rapidly spread across his face, but at that moment, I was just glad to have an ally. I had sold my soul to the devil. I believed my brother and everything that came out of his mouth.

Just as he had predicted, 'Ole Mousey kept to herself from that time on. She never again responded when she was called to come to the barn for milking or to be fed. Her milk production level dropped from about four gallons per milking to under a gallon. That was not sufficient enough to justify keeping a cow on a dairy farm. It cost too much to feed under-producing livestock. Dad made the decision to send 'Ole Mousey to market. He never could understand why all of a sudden she spiraled downward from being the best producer to being the worst. Lewis and I never offered any explanation nor speculation on the matter.

There are always cattle adventures on a dairy farm. We had a fifteen hundred pound bull that also had to be sent off to market for poor performance. He was extremely ill-tempered, and seemed to hate my mother. Whenever she went past the three-acre lot where the bull was kept, he would walk upright down the fence row with his front hooves on the top wire. He bellowed and snorted at her so ferociously that he would frighten Mom half to death. She always wanted Dad to get rid of him, but he was a true thoroughbred Guernsey and was too valuable for stud service to ever be sent away to market.

When the bull was being used for stud service, the cow had to be led by a rope and halter into the bull's lot so that when the mission had been accomplished, the cow could be led out again. Otherwise, you wouldn't be able to get the cow out of the lot. Either Dad or Lewis would lead the cow in and make sure she was turned in the right direction. The other would carry a cattle prod with which to back down the bull and a loaded rifle in case things went badly.

One day Dad decided to put an end to the bull's terrorism of Mom. We pulled the farm tractor with an attached dual wheel trailer into the Bull's lot with the intention of cutting off his horns and putting a brass ring with an attached lock chain into his nose. The lock chain would be long enough to drag the ground so that if he started to run, he would step on the chain. That would pull his head down, put a hurting in his nose, and slow him down in case he ever got out or got too rambunctious when he was being used for stud service.

I drove the tractor. Dad and Lewis rode on the trailer with the horn cutters and a brass nose ring with a three foot lock chain attached. As soon as we were in the lot where the bull was kept, he came charging and rammed the side of the trailer, shoving it sideways a couple of feet. The trailer was about ten feet long, six feet wide and had a flatbed made of one-inch solid oak boards attached to an all steel car frame. It had steel leaf springs over a tandem of rear axles from 1950's cars. The tongue that was attached to the tractor's tow bar was a hollow eight inch diameter quarter-inch thick steel casing that was approximately six feet long from tow bar to its attachment to the car frame.

That bull shouldered that trailer sideways like it were merely a child's Red Rider wagon. The snorting animal backed up a few feet and charged again. This time using his horns, he lifted the side of the trailer off the ground in an attempt to throw my brother and dad off.

He dropped the trailer and backed up for another charge. Hanging onto the headboard of the trailer with one hand, Dad tossed a lasso around the neck of the bull with his other hand and jumped off the back. He ran to a locust tree nearby and circled it with the rope three times.

Seeing where Dad had gone, the bull started around the back of the trailer to get him. When the bull charged around the trailer, Dad yelled for me to back up against the base of the tree. As the bull rounded the tree, Dad jumped back onto the trailer and I backed it up against the trunk of the tree as instructed. My dad and brother held onto the rope for dear life. With no slack in the rope and the trailer backed up against the tree, the bull was pinned on a "short rope."

Dad wrapped the end of the rope quickly around the headboard of the trailer so that Lewis would have enough leverage to hold onto the furious recalcitrant animal. Grabbing the horn cutters, Dad thrust them over the bull's left horn and squeezed with all the strength that he could muster. The base of the horn was at least four inches thick. Dad held onto the horn cutters for dear life. The bull pitched and cast his head up and down and side to side with such ferocity that Dad was tossed about as if he were a rag doll. Everything was happening much too fast. It appeared that the pertinacious bull could snap the ten-inch thick locust tree at any moment. Dad had no time to make any adjustments to the cutters even though they ended up being much too low.

Suddenly there was the sound of cracking and splintering. The cutters cut clean through the base of the tightly woven keratin that made up the horn. The infuriated bull jerked his head so violently that the cutters and the severed horn went flying to the ground ten feet away. Blood squirted from a severed artery in the base of the amputated horn with each beat of the raging beast's heart. In seconds the blood covered the trunk of the locust tree red as evenly as if a paint sprayer had been used.

More than being nefarious, the bull was now in pain. He leaped onto the bed of the trailer at the same time Dad and Lewis vaulted off onto the ground on the opposite side. Lewis held onto the rope tightly; it was cutting into the creature's neck. The defiant animal's air supply was slowly being cut off. His breath was hot and started coming in short bursts.

Blood spurted from the wound and snot bubbled from his nose. The bull's hooves seemed to go in four different directions. He could not stand up on the blood soaked oak boards of the trailer. He floundered about like a fish out of water and finally fell backward off the trailer onto the ground. Further enraged, the bull put his head down under the side of the trailer and once again lifted it a couple of feet off the ground in a desperate attempt to overturn what he must have considered his captor.

Even though the trailer weighed close to a thousand pounds, the provoked savage beast picked it up with his head as if it were no heavier than a bail of straw.

The sound of the ruckus could be heard all the way to the house, some three hundred yards away. Mom came out of the back door and yelled, "What in the world is going on down there? What are you all doing to that bull?"

Dad shouted to her to go back into the house and not come out again until he knew it was safe. Mom trusted Dad's instincts. Without another word and without question, she whirled around and went back into the house.

I remained on the seat of the tractor as if my pants were glued to it. Dad and Lewis danced about from behind the tree, behind the trailer, and from behind the rear tire of the tractor. Blood and snot covered the animal's face, neck and shoulders, and was smeared over the back of the trailer, the grass, and the side of the locust tree. Moment by moment the fury diminished. The animal was weakening from both exhaustion and loss of blood.

Finally the bull's legs buckled under him and he wobbled to the ground like a top running out of spin. Timing was everything. Dad jumped out from behind the rear tire of the tractor, opened the tool box attached to the inside of the rear fender of the tractor, removed a pair of pliers, and ran to the downed ungulate. He pushed the pliers down into the hollow stump of the severed horn and crushed the hemorrhaging artery. The fountain of blood that had already reduced to a trickle stopped all together. Dad removed a folded brown paper bag from the rear pocket of his work jeans, opened it, and took out a handful of sulfur. He packed the dried yellow powder into the hollow stump until it was even with the top of the bloody rim.

Dad tried in vain to loosen the rope from around the bull's neck, but it wouldn't budge. Once the rope had been lathered in blood and mucus, it became stiff as if glue had been poured over the knot and had hardened. Pulling a Tree Brand pocket knife from the front pocket of his Levi jeans, Dad cut the rope in two as easily as if it had been made of butter. He instructed Lewis to quickly bring him the brass nose ring with its attached lock chain. With his thumb and forefinger inside the animal's nostrils, Dad hoisted the bull's head up and as smooth as silk and as quickly as greased lightening, he inserted the brass nose ring. Once the sharp end of the open ring had penetrated the fleshy tissue of one nostril and had gone out the other side, Dad closed the ends together, inserted a small brass bolt, and quickly tightened the nut until it was flush with the side of the ring. He dropped the bull's head to the ground and stepped back like some rodeo calf-roper being timed at competition.

Dad instructed me to hand him a funnel and a canteen of water that swung from the tractor's taillight. He picked up the bull's head by the nose ring and shoved the tapered end of the funnel down the animal's throat. He uncorked the canteen and poured almost all the water into the nearly unconscious animal.

Dad stepped back and propped himself up by his elbows against the side of the trailer. Exhausted and overwhelmed from the excitement, Lewis plopped down on the trailer beside him, dangling his legs over the edge. I turned the tractor's engine off and swung around in the seat of the tractor. We sat there staring at the now docile beast. What a sight! The once fierce bull lay on the ground with his eyes rolled back in his head, heaving for every breath of air. What a sight! The once ferocious beast had the right horn cut off way too short and the left horn stuck straight out eighteen inches to the side. Talk about an uneven look! The one ton male ungulate's head and neck were covered in congealed blood, mingled with thick ropey snot. The corners of his mouth were outlined in foam and his nose was filled with bubbles. Mixed together they formed a pink froth that was sticky to the touch. The beast's eyes were red streaked from broken capillaries, making him look like an alcoholic who had been on a drunken binge for a week or two. His breathing was labored and mucus bubbled out his nostrils.

Our labored breathing from the altercation with the bull and the surge of adrenalin into our bloodstreams finally began to subside. Lewis and Dad climbed aboard the trailer; I turned around on the tractor seat and drove us out of the bull lot. We left the embattled creature behind on the ground to hopefully recover.

Recovering from the fear and exertion, I asked my dad, "Is he going to be alright?"

"I hope so, son," he answered. "He's mighty weak from the fight and the loss of blood. I sure pray to God he'll be alright."

Lewis or I would daily go by the bull's lot and check to see if he were still alive. He lay in the same spot for almost a week. Not once did we observe him try to stand up. One morning when I was on my way to the barn, I noticed that the bull was no longer down by the locust tree. As a matter of fact, I didn't see him anywhere.

I dropped the bucket of hot water that I was carrying to the barn to wash off the cow's utters and ran back to the house. When I came around the corner of the granary I saw the bull in his lot at the corner of the yard. He was standing before an old white porcelain bathtub that we used as a watering trough. He seemed to be swaying a little but he was taking in gulp after gulp of water.

I thought that it might be a good idea to feed him some ground corn with sweet molasses. It was a mixture that had lots of minerals added, the same concoction that we fed to the cows while they were being milked. I ran to the barn, got a three gallon bucket and filled it half full of the enriched corn mixture. I returned to the rear of the house and climbed up onto the fence that surrounded the yard. Leaning over as far as I could without tumbling over into the lot with the bull, I placed the bucket onto the ground in front of the beast. He sniffed it and then began to gobble it up. He certainly must have been famished after not eating for a week.

For a month or so that bull kept quiet. He ate grass, drank his water, but never again walked the fence bellowing at Mom. Once in awhile, I'd see him come to the tub for water. Sometimes he would step on the lock chain that would pull his head down. He'd stop, back up to get off the chain, and lift his head higher so he wouldn't let that happen again.

At the breakfast table one Saturday morning, Dad asked Lewis and me if we had seen the bull. He said that Mom had mentioned to him that she had not seen him for at least three days. "Would you boys go around the lot and make sure he hasn't gotten out. He may just be in the patch of pines at the rear of the lot, but you better make sure."

"Sure Dad," we replied, happy that we could help.

After we finished eating, Lewis and I put on our baseball caps and went to check on the bull. We had just about circled the entire field when we saw the bull standing, facing the fence at the back of the patch of black pines. We approached him from outside his lot and noticed that he didn't move one little bit. When we were square in front of the bull, we realized that the lock chain that was attached to his nose ring was draped over the electric wire that ran the perimeter of the field. The current was mild enough to not have electrocuted him but strong enough that it had sapped him of all his strength. He stood there unable to back up and free himself.

Lewis picked up a dead pine tree limb that was lying on the ground and carefully lifted the chain off the wire. The bull just stood there. He was too weak to move.

Using the same dead pine limb, Lewis whacked the dazed creature across his one remaining horn to startle him into moving. He backed up a couple of feet, but it was like he was moving in slow motion. He was trying to moo, but he could only wheeze.

He eventually recovered from the electric fence incident, but became so docile that he was worthless as a stud animal and had to be shipped off to the market. In my young mind, I surmised that being responsible for 'Ole Mousey's diminished output of milk was equaled by Dad being responsible for the best stud bull we ever had developing E.D.

I informed my brother that his ownership of me was over. My deed was no worse than what he and Dad had done to that bull. I told him not to think that because I was there I had anything to do with the downfall of that great beast. I was only there driving the tractor for their safety. My words must have done some good. He never tried to blackmail me with 'Ole Mousey after that. Through the years, there were plenty of other things worthy of "blackmail", of course.

Chapter Nine

Stitches, Witches, and Switches

Many times I wanted to play instead of help Lewis with the milking chores. One time he came out the backdoor and yelled for me to come help him bring in the cows for milking. I didn't respond. Lewis noticed that something was rustling under the stalks of corn that filled the trailer parked in the open stall of the granary. He surmised that I had crawled in underneath the fodder to hide. He continued to call for me to come out to help him while he gathered a few rocks out of the unpaved driveway. Pretending that he had not seen where I was hiding, Lewis nonchalantly started throwing rocks first at the shed to make a loud racket and then at the fodder. I couldn't stand it any longer. I raised my head up above the corn stalks to see where my brother was at the same instant that he released a rock that was just smaller than a baseball. "Crack!" That rock caught me right between the eyes. Lewis could see from where he was standing that my eyes rolled upward until only the whites of my eyes showed. I fell out of that trailer to the ground like a sack of potatoes rolling off the back of a truck.

Lewis rushed to where I had fallen and rolled me over. My face was covered in blood and a small spurt kept shooting up rhythmically from between my eyes. I was unconscious. Lewis lowered my head back onto the ground and ran to the house to get Mom. Raising two boys that were so often out of control, he knew that she would know exactly what to do.

When Lewis told her what had happened, she didn't panic, and she didn't even ask a million questions like, "what have you done?" She simply grabbed a clean towel out of the bathroom linen closet and ran out the back door. Ignoring what she preached to us so many times about letting the screen door slam when we ran out of the house, she let it slam hard behind her.

When she reached my unconscious limp body, Mom placed the clean towel over the artery that spurted blood onto the petite flower-patterned cotton dress she had made from chop sacks. She wiped the blood away from the stone-inflicted wound, and started slapping me gently across the face. I aroused momentarily and asked, "What hit me?"

After I opened my eyes and spoke, Lewis' heart beat normally for the first time since before he had "cold-cocked" me with the rock. He was so relieved to see me move again, and to know that he hadn't killed me that he started to cry. Mom thought that he was crying out of fear and remorse and turned around to console him. He didn't know how that made me feel, but it made him feel great.

Lewis truly would not have wanted to hurt or maim me in any way, even though there was always this unspoken rivalry for Mon's affections between us.

It was actually incredible how Mom handled the situation without panic. Pressing the towel firmly against the artery spurting blood, she helped me to my feet, and walked me to the car. She turned to Lewis and said, "You will have to take care of the milking and feeding by yourself. I have to take Larry to Dr. Porter's office in town."

Town was nine miles away. Lewis watched Mom drive away with me in the seat beside her. I sat there with my head reclined back on the headrest. After we were out of sight, my brother walked slowly through the barnyard and over the hill behind the barn to drive the cows in for milking.

We must have been gone two or three hours. When we returned, Lewis was still in the shed that had the new-born calves in it, milking the cows after the calves had gotten their fill of fresh milk. I went to the barn to find Lewis, to show him the "red badge of courage" that

I sported. After closing the wound with three or four stitches, the Doctor had placed a bandage across my nose between my eyes in the form of an "X". When I opened the barn door and stuck my head in, Lewis saw the "X" bandage.

He had been sitting on a three-legged stool milking a cow, and had been crying his eyes out ever since Mom and I had left for the doctor's office in town. Upon seeing me, Lewis stopped his crying and started to laugh. He laughed so hard that he nearly fell off the stool. Part of the laughter was relief from seeing that I was alright and part for the shear comedy of the bandage.

Lewis had the audacity to say to me that since he had cried so much, his sinuses that had been clogged for over a week had now drained and he wanted to thank me for that. I could have just slapped him. However, restraint was the wiser choice. I had not yet exceeded him in size.

* * * * * *

Dad had a relative, Uncle Price, whom <u>everyone</u> called "uncle" whether they were related to him or not. He was a stern man, a Primitive Baptist preacher by avocation. With a frame slight as a willow, he came walking into church on Sunday mornings with his back straight and his head held high. He would approach the pulpit with perfect posture and a noticeable hint of arrogance. He always wore a pin-striped black worsted wool suit with a buttoned-up vest (save for the bottom button), black "old men's" shoes, and he carried a black bola in his right hand. He put it on only after the service was over. He didn't want to muss his perfectly groomed snow white hair. A gold chain hung across the front of his vest. It was attached at one end to the middle buttonhole of his vest and the other end to a gold pocket watch placed carefully in the left vest pocket.

His sermons were strong expository messages, mostly from the Old Testament. Hell was a common topic and the wrath of God the theme. He was a stereotypical old-timey pure "hellfire and damnation" preacher. I'm not implying that there was anything wrong with that, it's just that it was his only sermon theme.

Uncle Price was married to a very petite woman. At best she was probably no more than five feet, three inches tall with a tiny waist, narrow shoulders, and small feet. As best as I can remember, she always wore black. She rarely, if ever, came to church with her preacher-husband.

Dad really liked this uncle. He admired him for his preaching, his superb posture, and his mental acuity, intact well into his nineties. We often visited with him and his wife. The entertainment for the adults was simply conversation, for Lewis and me it was anything we could find to amuse ourselves with in the front yard.

During one visit, Dad had stopped at the Nester store near our home and had bought rolls of caps for Lewis and me to use in our Roy Rogers cap pistols. After burning through a couple of rolls, the springs on both of our pistols slipped from their attachments and stopped working. We started exploding the caps on the front steps of Uncle Price's house with small rocks found in the drainage ditch in front of his house.

Even that became boring after awhile. Lewis discovered that by holding a roll of caps between the side of the index finger and the tip of the nail of the thumb, and quickly flicking the bubble filled with powder, the powder inside the bubble would discharge with a flash.

We had exploded three or four rolls of caps in this manner when there was a back-flash of powder that burned the skin on the end of my thumb and scorched my nail black. The discoloration could not be rubbed off and the pain in my thumb was intense. After sucking on my thumb and rubbing the burned area vigorously, I finally had to go into the house and confess to my mother what had happened. O course I went in crying so I would get less scolding and more sympathy.

Lewis told Mom and Dad what had happened and how the end of my thumb had been burned in the process. I went running to Mom so she could kiss my "boo boo," but it didn't seem to help. The burning sensation was still there and getting worse. Everyone was trying to do something but nothing was lessening my pain, let alone my anxiety.

Finally, Uncle Price's wife said to me, "Come here child and let Elvira look at that."

There was a strange calmness to her voice. Usually I would have let no one except my mother look at my wound, but her words and the way in which she said them eased my distress.

I slipped off my mother's lap and walked over to where Elvira sat in an old winged-back Queen Anne chair. She put her hands around my waist and hoisted me up onto her lap. She took my thumb in her hand and closed her fingers around it tightly. Closing her eyes, she mumbled something under her breath and instantly the pain was gone.

Aunt Elvira opened her eyes and pushed me off her lap onto the floor. I stood there with my mouth hanging open in amazement. She said to me softly, "That will take care of your pain, sweetheart. I removed the fire, but I'm afraid your thumbnail will remain black until it grows out."

Without any other comment, Dad instructed me to thank her, and I did.

The cold chill that went up and down my spine remained. I started to ask her if she were a witch, but realizing what I was about to say,

Dad quickly cut me off. "Elvira is a kind woman, isn't she, Larry? How good of her to remove the fire from your thumb."

I just stood there staring at her and muttered as if I were a zombie, "Yes, she is a very kind woman."

Mom reached out and pulled me to her. She hugged me tightly and kissed me on the forehead. The firmness of her hug told me to say no more. In about half an hour Dad announced that we needed to get going. The cows had to be brought in, fed, and milked.

We said our goodbyes and I clung to Mom's dress as if I were part of it. When we got to the car, she pulled me free and opened the rear door for Lewis and me to pile in.

Once we had left their driveway, Lewis and I started firing our questions. "Is she a witch, Daddy? Is she a witch? Can she do other magic? Can she cast spells? Has she ever used her magic for bad? Is that why she doesn't go to church?"

"Whoa, slow down you two," Dad said with a chuckle. "We don't call Elvira a witch. She's an 'enchantress.' I don't know if she can perform other 'magic' or not. What I do know is that she can remove the sting and pain from burns in a matter of seconds. Whether she casts spells or not, I don't know."

Mom began laughing and then made the comment, "Everyone has always said that she got Uncle Price to marry her by casting a spell on him."

"That's not true, Violet," Dad objected. "I've heard that too, but Uncle Price married her because he loved her. It's as simple as that."

"She is one strange bird, if you ask me," Mom added. "She never goes anywhere with Uncle Price. She never goes to church, nor is she very sociable. You never see the two of them together outside their home. And when we come to visit she spends most of the time in the kitchen getting us something to drink and eat."

"Now that certainly is suspicious," Dad mocked. "A woman who spends her time serving her guests food and drink. Why that puts her in line to be burned at the stake."

"Stop it, Carbin," Mom said sternly. "You know what I'm talking about. It's not the making or the serving of the food and drinks that's the problem; it's that she spends practically the entire visit in the kitchen. She comes into the parlor just long enough to bring each person the goodies and to take away the dishes and glasses. The rest of the time she spends almost entirely in the kitchen."

Dad replied laughing, "I know what you're saying. I was just teasing you. She _is_ a strange one, quiet and withdrawn. She never enters into any conversation voluntarily. She's the perfect church mouse."

"I don't know about the church part," Mom interjected. "The mouse part I'll grant you. She gives me the willies sometimes, that's all."

"Me too," I added. "She scares me."

"Scared or not, Larry, she made the hurt go away, didn't she?" Dad asked.

"Yes, she made the pain go away," I answered, "but she made me feel so cold all over, and the chill hasn't gone away yet."

"It will," Dad said. "She took the pain out of a burn for me when I was a child and I felt icy cold all over for the rest of the day. The cold eventually subsided, but not as quickly as the pain from the burn. For that we can be grateful, witch or not."

That was a truth on which we could hang our hats. Silence became the byword for the remainder of the trip home. The witch/enchantress Elvira was not mentioned again.

* * * * * *

There was yet another "witch" that was related to us, related again by marriage of course. That was a lady in our neighborhood by the name of Laura.

When I was about five or six years old the phone company came through our part of the state installing phone lines. We were able to have our first telephone installed. Many people will not know or remember this, but the first phones installed had to be on party lines. There was no such thing as a private line. Our first phone had twelve families sharing the same phone line. When someone's phone would ring, the eleven other phones would vibrate. Everyone always knew if someone in the group was getting a call.

Laura was an infamous eavesdropper. It got to the point that when you were finished talking to someone that had called you, not only would you say goodbye to the party to whom you had been speaking, but also to Laura. She never thought to cover the receiver with the palm of her hand. You could always hear her breathing as she listened in. So when you said, "Good bye so and so, and oh, good bye Laura," you would hear her put her phone into its cradle. It got to be quite a joke. You certainly did not say anything to anyone that you did not want Laura to hear or repeat.

One sunny summer afternoon Dad constructed a fire pit underneath an old apple tree in the side yard. He made the pit five or six rows of brick high using some old ones that had been stacked for several years in the backyard. Dad placed a metal grate from an old discarded stove on top of the bricks.

I don't remember the occasion, but people were at our house for a cookout. Dad had started a fire in the pit using charcoal briquettes, and had covered it with the metal grate. When he had finished cooking all the hamburgers and hotdogs, Dad took the red hot metal grate off the makeshift fire pit and threw it to the side to cool.

Several young children my age had come to the cookout with their parents and we were running barefoot hither and yon, playing the game of tag. I didn't see the hot grate lying hidden in the grass and ran across it. The pain to the bottom of my foot was instant. I fell to the ground, grabbed my burning foot, and began to wail loudly.

My mother ran to me and began to access the situation. She knelt down by my side, lifted the foot that I was nursing, and inspected the injury. Across the bottom of the one foot that had come in contact with the grate were half a dozen black stripes. She turned and looked at the grate lying on the ground beside me and discovered half a dozen rods with my flesh sticking to them.

I held my foot and rolled over and over in the grass screaming. I had never felt such intense pain in my young life. The pain that I experienced when I burned the end of my thumb with the cap was nothing compared to this. The bottom of my foot where the skin and muscle underneath had been instantly cooked and pulled away was "on fire." I cannot imagine the excruciating pain a victim from a house fire must experience. Mine was bad enough.

Mom ran into the house and brought out some honey and rubbed it all over the sole of my burnt foot. I wasn't sure if she were trying to soothe the burn or baste me for further roasting. In any case, it didn't help. I was still in agony.

Dad took charge and said, "I'm going into the house and call Laura."

Again my thoughts were on the wild side. 'Is Dad calling her so that as the local gossip she can spread the news? She lives right next door to the local country store, is he calling her to bring some salt to rub on my wounds? What is he thinking?'

My parents were unable to console me. The pain was getting worse and they were calling for someone to come, someone who listened to our every word spoken on the phone. After what seemed like an eternity, Laura finally arrived and ran to where I lay on the ground twisting and turning from the burning pain in the bottom of my foot.

She immediately dropped to her knees beside me and like my great Uncle Price's wife, took my injured foot into the palm of her hand, closed her hand around it and closed her eyes. She said some mumbo jumbo words under her breath and in an instant, the burning sensation was gone. Not only was the burning gone, all pain had vanished.

My parents took her aside and thanked her for coming to my aid. I think they gave her some money, but I can't be sure. I was able to run and jump with the other children for the rest of the day.

Not only was the pain still gone the next day, but there were no signs of the burn stripes on the bottom of my foot. The area was completely healed.

I know as Christians we should never deal in the occult or contact witches or soothsayers, but as a child in pain, I didn't care. These two "friendly witches" had the power somehow to take the fire out and heal my burns.

* * * * * *

It seems as though I got a spanking or a switching every other day of my life until I was eleven years old. I don't know if that is the official cut off date or whether I finally wised up. Part of my punishments were earned and deserved, others were not. However, many of them were as a result of being set up by my older brother.

When we were young, Lewis was always harassing me. He had a habit of smacking me on one side of the face then on the other, back and forth. He didn't hurt me, just annoyed and aggravated me.

Lewis would try to get me to do something for him, like milk the cows, feed them in his stead, mow the yard, or something. Whenever I didn't give him the desired response, he would go to Mom and tell her that I wasn't doing my part. I wasn't milking the cows after he had fed them, or I was supposed to trim the yard with the push mower after he had used the riding mower. I never knew exactly who said that if he did one thing I was expected to do the other, but it worked out that way. Since he was the older and "wiser" one, I got the punishment on his say so.

When Lewis and I were preteens, he was chubby and I was thin. That was certainly a God thing, because being smaller I could outrun him and most of the time stay clear of any vengeance that might be coming my way.

Many times I would do something that would irritate him and he would want to punish me for it. As he reached for me, I would start backing away, turn, and then outrun him. A white board fence about four feet high surrounded the yard of our house. When my brother chased after me, I would run for the fence. I could do what we would now dub an "Air Jordan." Leaping into the air, I would hit the top board of the fence with my stomach, flip over to the other side of the fence and keep running. Lewis, on the other hand, would have to stop, climb up and over the fence. The majority of time when he was about halfway over the fence he would realize that catching me really wasn't worth it (he wasn't going to catch me anyway), and he would give up. Of course I knew the time of retribution was ahead and I would eventually receive my "reward," whether earned or not.

* * * * * *

Living on a farm can be dirty business. Boys notoriously enjoy being dirty, and what better place than growing up on a farm. Consequently, Lewis and I were often dirty. However, Mom had this funny quirk; she wanted and expected her boys to be clean and remain so. She would clean us up, dress us in fresh clothes, open the door to a dirty world, and tell us, "Go out and play, but don't get dirty." That's like Brear Rabbit saying to the fox, "Don't throw me into that briar patch."

When we were younger, the quarter mile drive from our house to the highway was in fact a dirt road. If the season had been rainy, the ditches on either side of the drive were filled with water, a perfect place to sail wooden boats or stomp the muddy water until the entire driveway was wet. If the driveway were wet, we were certainly wet as well.

Our well went dry one year and Dad hired my Grandfather's well drilling company to come and sink a new well. Grandpa's crew built a v-shaped trough that led from the hole being drilled to an area about twenty feet away. Water was pumped from storage barrels into the drilling hole to keep the drill bits cooled. This was supposed to prevent them from binding or breaking. The wooden trough carried away the excess water mixed with the dirt being removed from the hole being drilled. That combination made the best mudslide imaginable.

As usual, Lewis and I were sent out to play in clean clothes and warned to stay away from the drilling site. ("Don't throw me into that briar patch!") When we saw that thick muddy water running down that trough, it was more temptation than little boys could possibly resist. It didn't take more than fifteen minutes before we climbed into the trough at the top and enjoyed the ride on our backs to the bottom. After we had taken four or five runs our mother came out of the house to check on us. When she spotted us sliding down the trough, she came running. She yelled for us to get out of that mud.

The only logical way down was to slide on our backs to the bottom one more time. Mom was livid. She grabbed each one of us by the arm and dragged us from the mud. With one open-handed swat to each of our rear ends, she sent us packing toward the house. She then turned on her dad and her brother who were working the drilling equipment and screamed at them, "Why did you let the boys get in that mud? You know better than that! What is wrong with you two? You are just about as bad as Lewis and Larry!"

Before they had a chance to respond or defend themselves, Mom whirled around and marched like a toy soldier on a mission back to the house. She came around the corner of the house and found her two little darlings covered from head to toe in yellowish brown mud. We were standing by an aluminum washtub that was filled with water warmed by the sun waiting for our dear mother.

The mud was caked to our clothes and to our skin as tenaciously as a shell to the back of a tortoise. Mom was furious. Her frustration came from the fact that this was not the first time that she had told us not to get into that very mud. She wanted to get on us like flees on a dog, but, because she was so mad, decided to delay any action.

As if she had conceived the proper punishment for disobeying her, she said to us, "I want the two of you to go to the hickory tree on the fence line between our farm and the Cunduff farm and bring me a hickory switch. It is to be approximately the same diameter as the radio antenna on your father's Studebaker, and I want all the leaves and little limbs striped away. Do you understand?"

We answered like perfect children, "Yes Mother."

We never, but never called her "Mother," but when you have just pushed the envelope to the limit, you want to be as respectful as humanly possible.

The hickory tree that Mom sent us to for her switch was about two football field lengths east of the house. As had happened numerous times before, we cried all the way to fetch the switch. When we reached the hickory tree that was on the boundary between the two properties, Lewis climbed the wire fence to break off one of the auxiliary limbs that fit the description of the switch that Mom had given to us. Once he had broken it off, he striped the sprouts and the leaves away. What was left was a thin flexible shaft that gave off a whipping sound when it was snapped back and forth.

With the specified switch in hand, we resumed our crying and walked back to the house. When we reached the porch, Mom was sitting on the top step waiting for us. Lewis handed her the hickory switch and stepped back. We both kept our heads down and our eyes looking at the ground in a display of submission.

She took the switch from Lewis and said, "You boys take your clothes off and stand over by the wash tub."

Knowing what was coming, we did as we were told. It took a Watkins horsehair brush to scrub all the mud off our bodies and out of our hair. Once we were finished, we were marched into the house to the bedroom we shared. There Mom redressed us in clean clothes and instructed us to go set the table for dinner. The three of us went to the kitchen. Mom took the everyday dishes from a white metal cabinet that stood on the floor beside the kitchen table and handed half of them to Lewis and the other half to me. She laid the hickory switch on top of the refrigerator and said not another word about giving us the lashes we so rightly deserved.

It happened that way with some degree of frequency. Sometimes, when we brought the requested switch to her, she would apply it several times to the back of our legs. Other times she would lay it up for another time. And there were always other times.

A hickory switch like that would last a very long time. But when there had been no need of it for several days, either Lewis or I would sneak into the kitchen and remove the instrument of punishment from atop of the refrigerator. One of us would take the switch out back and dispose of it. Fortunately Mom never caught us in the act. That would have been certain grounds for a few lashes across our naked legs. She knew that we were the ones who had taken the hickory switch, but she never said anything about it. Sending us for a new switch, whether it was used then or later, was part of our punishment, and it seemed to have worked as planned.

Chapter Ten

Sick of Christmas

Unlike today when the Christmas tree is the focus of attention, the Christmas trees that we had as children could be described as no other than a "Charlie Brown Christmas tree." We were never ever certain if Dad did what he did intentionally or if he really had no sense of what a full, beautiful tree looked like. About a week before Christmas arrived, Dad would go to the "white building," remove the ax from its hook from behind the door, and ride his gray and red Ford farm tractor over the hill to the back of our farm where lots of white pine trees grew. When he returned with his freshly cut tree, his "bounty" was always absolutely pitiful. He would swear up and down to Mom that he had looked and looked for the best tree, but unless you count a misshapen shrub, this was the best that could be found. There could have been a problem with his story. One time he came in with a tree that was about three feet high, had a diameter of about two inches at the base, and had a total of six limbs, not one that opposed another.

He first squared off the bottom of the tree with a handsaw and then nailed two pine boards together in the shape of an X. He screwed these to the bottom of the tree for its base. It was up to Mom to make this thing beautiful. That was never going to happen.

She went into the closet and dragged out an old cardboard hatbox decorated with pink roses that had faded so badly that the flowers were barely discernable. All the tree decorations that she and Dad had ever owned were in it. The silver tinsel that she draped around the tree had been used for so many years that it was compacted down to about a half inch in diameter instead of the three inch one it had once been. All the glittering effects of the silver decorative foil had totally lost its luster. There were a dozen two-inch glass balls of four different colors that she hung in no particular pattern on the tiny limbs. Some of the colored enamel was either worn away or chipped away on each and every glass ornament, so that you could actually see the wire clip inside the spherical ball by which it was hung. All the limbs of the abashed tree were bent downward from the weight of the twelve balls until they all nearly touched the floor. Lewis and I were allowed to toss hands full of silver icicles that had been used on several prior Christmas trees onto the fallen limbs. Because they were so crinkled, they resembled cat's whiskers that had come too close to an open flame, sticking out in all directions.

Mom prepared six packages exactly alike. She wrapped each gift in tissue thin green paper decorated with a red Christmas tree pattern. Next she ran a red corrugated ribbon up each side of the boxes and tied the ends of the ribbons together on top, leaving the ends of the ribbon six inches long. After making bows by looping pieces of ribbon six times and tying them together with a short piece of ribbon, she attached them to the packages by the ends she had left sticking up. These she curled using the side of a pair of scissors. Cutting name tags from white typing paper, Mom wrote each person's name on their tag and taped them to the presents. There was a present from Mom to Dad and one from him to her, a present for Theoa, one for Mo, one for Lewis, and one for me.

Finally my mother placed the look-alike gifts under the sad evergreen. Even the color of the pine needles wasn't right. They were a washed out pale green instead of the vibrant forest green one would expect. Besides the wrapped presents each one in the family received a see-through stocking made of crosshatch vinyl that was filled with oranges, apples, nuts in the shell, candy canes, and either a small box of Brach's chocolate covered cherries or a handful of licorice or Werner's butterscotch.

We would always have a two pound fruitcake in a tin that had a picture of Scrooge carrying Tiny Tim on his shoulder. The hosiery mill where Dad worked gave each of their employees one for Christmas. Additionally, there would be a box of stick candy of different flavors, a crate of grapefruit, a crate of oranges, and a wooden bowl filled with mixed nuts in their shells. The nut bowl contained a nut cracker and a couple of "nut pickers" and set on the coffee table for everyone to enjoy.

There were four straight Christmases that were no fun for me and I am sure that I made it miserable for everyone else as well. I had to be a medical anomaly because there are two types of measles, rubeola and rubella. Supposedly, once you had each kind of measles, you developed immunity to them and wouldn't suffer either again.

Three Christmases in a row I had the measles, rubeola one year and rubella the next two, or visa versa, I don't remember which. In the fourth year following these three miserable Christmases I came down with the mumps. Is that any way for a kid to have to celebrate the birth of Christ?

That first Christmas when I came down with a case of the measles, my parents let me open my present early in an attempt to cheer me up. It was a Roy Rogers Ranch set, complete with plastic figurines of Roy, his wife Dale Evans, a goofy sidekick known as Pat and his Army jeep, a handful of ranch hands, a bunkhouse, a barn, some cattle, Roy's horse Trigger, Dale's horse Buttermilk, ranch hand horses, saddles, bridles, and enough fencing to surround the entire shooting match. I always wondered why there was no main house. Naively, at age eight I figured Roy and Dale just stayed in the bunk house with their men.

Even though I was hot with fever, itched all over, had watery burning eyes, and all my muscles ached, I would lie in the floor next to the coal burning stove that heated the den and dining area and played as long as I could before falling asleep. Mom would simply cover me up with a blanket where I lay. After all, it was nice and warm there.

The following Christmas: *déjà vu.* I had the measles again, the other kind. Mom and Dad let me open my present a week early again. This time it was a castle that was complete with a drawbridge, king, queen, knights, horses, trolls, and a whole box full of Druid foot soldiers with swords and long bows. There were at least thirty battles before Christmas day even arrived.

I was a little better about sharing at age nine than I was at eight. This time I allowed Lewis to enjoy my gift as well. After all, it was more fun for someone else to attack the castle than to have to attack it myself only to turn around and have to defend it.

By the time I had recovered from the measles, all the fun had gone out of the castle. I started having the Druid foot soldiers attack

Roy and Dale's ranch and drive off their cattle. Then it became theirs and their ranch hands' responsibility to protect the king and the queen. That didn't seem too much of a stretch to me, however, the sidekick driving his Army jeep into battle against the Druids might have been a little much.

It must be "Groundhog Day!" A few years ago a movie hit the theatres starring Bill Murray. The name of the flick was *Groundhog Day*. Every morning when Bill's character was awakened by the alarm clock going off, he would start the day exactly as he had the day before, and the entire day would be a replication of the previous day. He was living the same day over and over and over. When, for the third year in a row, I came down with a case of the measles (when everyone knows that there are only two types of the virus), I could have been Bill Murray living in *"Groundhog Day."* I couldn't believe it, my parents couldn't believe it, and certainly the family doctor couldn't.

Dad asked Dr. Cox if he were absolutely certain that I had had the measles the previous two Christmases. After a barrage of curse words for having his diagnosis questioned, his answer was a definite affirmative. Having either rubeola or rubella again went against all medical knowledge (at that time); however, there was no doubt in the doctor's mind that I was yet again having one of them. It must have been that I had not developed a sufficient quantity of antibodies against the form of measles that I had indeed contracted once more. To a ten year old, the whole thing seemed to be an impossibility. Both times that I had had the measles, I was covered with the small dark pink macules, displayed the high fever, the watering eyes, the aching in all my muscles, and the headache that formed across my forehead. The doctor may have been mistaken, but my symptoms certainly were not. I had had both rubeola and rubella, and here I was having one of them again.

Just like the previous two Christmases, Mom and Dad allowed me to open my present early. And like the two previous ones, I opened a present that was full of little men. This time my present was a squadron of army figures posed in at least four different positions: riflemen on their stomachs, men on one knee with a bazooka on their shoulders, men holding rifles with attached bayonets in an advancing pose, and at least two commanders looking through field glasses. There were jeeps pulling canons, Army trucks with fabric canopies over their beds, pup tents, and of course, a stiff American flag made to look like it was blowing in the wind high on a flag pole. Thing was, everything was forest green, including the soldiers' faces. When you're ten, however, your imagination can compensate for such little issues.

Lewis must have thought that I was having the measles every Christmas just so I could open my present early. I can assure you that having little itchy macules, eyes that constantly water and burn when you are in a bright light, having a constant headache over your eyes, and aching over your entire body twenty-four hours a day is not my idea of something one would intentionally do in order to open one lousy Christmas present early. It just wasn't worth it!

To top things off, the following Christmas I had the mumps. A week before the celebration of the blessed event, there was a family that came to visit us one evening. They had two children, a girl my brother's age, and a girl my age. Lewis and his new friend went off by themselves; they were "too big" and "too old" for us. After my friend and I had exhausted playing all the games that we could think of to play, we started jumping up and down on the guest bed. No one caught us and therefore there was no punishment for abusing the furniture.

About eleven o'clock the guests took their two daughters and left. My family retired for the evening. When I got up the next morning, I could hardly swallow. The area in front of my right ear was swollen slightly and was sore to the touch. I came to the breakfast table, not my usual self. I was listless. I couldn't even eat. Finally Mom asked, "Larry, what is wrong with you? You haven't touched any of the food on your plate. There are starving children in the world and we don't take food we do not intend to eat."

"Then send this food to those starving children," I barked. "I don't want it."

You would have thought that I had just cursed God! Mom, Dad, and Lewis sucked in air in disbelief and simultaneously murmured, "Uhh oooh!"

"What did you just say, young man," my dad asked? "You don't talk to your mother that way, and just as importantly, you don't think like that."

"Yeah! Whatever," I said. I laid my head down on the table beside my plate.

Normally I would never have back-talked my mother, to say nothing of my dad. Then not to have apologized but to have added to the sin that I had already committed would have bordered on the unpardonable in our home.

Dad reached down and unbuckled the belt around his waist and very slowly pulled it through all the belt loops. In a display of authority, he laid one end of the wide leather belt out on the linoleum floor in front of me and said, "Let me ask you one more time, is that any way to talk to your mother?"

I never lifted my head off the table, but answered just above a whisper, "Whatever!"

"Whatever!" my dad bellowed. With a glaze over his eyes and a definite intent in his voice, he screamed, "I'll show you whatever!"

Dad pushed his chair back from the table with the back of his legs so forcibly that the chair tilted over backwards and crashed to the floor. He hardly ever lost his temper, but he definitely came around the table for me. As he stretched forth his hand to grab hold of my arm, Mom put up her hand and stopped him in his tracks.

"Carbin!" she yelled sternly, "this is not how your son normally acts, now is it?"

"No," my dad answered angrily." Pointing to me, he continued, "but he…"

"But nothing," Mom said. "There's something wrong with the boy, which doesn't call for any kind of punishment!"

"Is something hurting you, Baby?" Mom asked me with empathy. "Does your tummy hurt?"

Disgruntled, I answered, "No."

"Then what is it?" Mom asked patiently.

"I don't feel well; I feel hot!" I replied holding my face in my hands. "My throat hurts and my right ear hurts too."

Dad had been waiting to swat me, but instead, walked away from the table and went into the kitchen, putting his belt back on as he went.

Mom yelled after him, "Where are you going?"

Dad didn't answer. He returned momentarily holding a dill pickle in his right hand. He shoved the pickle in front of my face and said, "Here, take a bite of this."

"I don't want to," I said through pouting lips.

"Do as I tell you, Larry," Dad instructed, "or so help me, sick or not, I'll give you some of my leather belt."

"Carbin!" Mom growled like a momma bear protecting her cub. "Don't you dare lay a hand on him."

Dad just looked at Mom as if to say, 'You know I would not.'

He held the pickle in front of me. I raised my aching head off the table and took a bite of the pickle as I had been instructed.

There was a searing pain in my cheek in front of my right ear. I cringed, closed my eyes together tightly, made an awful face, and spit out the chunk of pickle that I had just bitten off. I grabbed the right side of my face and cried out, "Ouch! That hurts!"

"Just as I suspected," Dad said triumphantly. "He has the mumps!"

"The mumps?" Mom repeated. She pulled me into her arms, and looked up at Dad standing beside her and asked, "Are you sure he has the mumps, Carbin?"

He folded his arms like "Mr. Clean" from the detergent commercials and answered, "Yep! A sure sign of the mumps is to take a bite of a sour pickle and if it hurts real badly in front of the ear, you've got your diagnosis!"

The mumps! I couldn't believe it. Four years in a row I was going to be sick at Christmas! At least it was not the measles. Oh nooooo.... it's the mumps!

By the afternoon my face had puffed up in front of my right ear so much so that I resembled a chipmunk holding an acorn in his cheek. To my horror, my right testicle was also swollen and was so painful that I could hardly stand up. I was so embarrassed, but I had to tell Mom about that development, I had no choice. I needed to go to the bathroom, but I couldn't stand up from the pain in my groin. Dad had left for work already and having no options, I told my mother of my dilemma.

Mom called Doctor Cox and told him of this latest development. He said that I would have to stay in bed flat on my back. I would have to use a bed pan whenever I needed to go to the bathroom, and a pillow should be placed under my buttocks and another under my swollen testicle to help support it. If it were allowed to hang down, I might pull something loose and besides the pain would become unbearable.

Were they kidding me? Your testicles swell up when you get the mumps? I couldn't believe it! Not only was I sick with a viral illness for the fourth Christmas in a row, one of my family jewels had swollen so large that I could not stand up and to make matters worse, I had to lay on my back with a pillow under it. Any pressure on that one "bad boy" from hanging down whatsoever made both my testacies hurt like I had been kicked in the groan repeatedly.

Another Christmas being sick! I had to lie on the sofa in the den where the room was heated, have a pillow placed under my scrotum for support, and I could not have a blanket over me because any pressure on my swollen testicle was too painful. Besides, I was just too hot. I felt ruined! I was undone! Was there anything else that might befall me? Maybe the ceiling would collapse on me and just put an end to my misery!

"Why?" I asked my mother who was standing beside the sofa where I had laid down. "How can this be? I was just playing with Carrie last night."

"I know son," she said sympathetically. "Sometimes it just doesn't make any sense. Doctor Cox said that your mumps have 'fallen' on you, which means that now you have the mumps in the salivary gland in your right jaw and in one of your testicles."

"That's preposterous," I said.

"Well," Mom responded shaking her head, "it seems that you had the mumps last night. You just didn't have any symptoms then. With the mumps you are to remain still, for if you don't, they can 'fall' on you. And the place they fall to is exactly where you have the swelling now. For example, if you and Carrie were to have jumped up and down on the bed last night, and if you already had the mumps, all that jumping could cause the virus to migrate downward."

"Well, isn't that just grand," I moaned. "Just how long are my family jewels to remain this size, Mom?"

"I'm not entirely sure, Larry," she replied, answering me as only a loving mother could. "Dr. Cox said that the mumps last somewhere between eleven to fourteen days."

"Eleven to fourteen days!" I screamed. I began to cry and mumbled, "You mean to tell me that I have to lie here flat of my back for eleven to fourteen days! I can't get up and go to the bathroom, and on top of that I have to keep a pillow under my family jewels to boot?"

"That seems to be the case," my loving mother replied. "I'm sorry son, but that's the way the cookie crumbles."

I would have shaken my head in disgust or in disbelief, but any movement of my head hurt too much. I was too sick and it was too painful for me to have any movement. Instead of getting my Christmas present early, I didn't get to open it for two whole weeks. What a miserable Christmas, more so than the previous three!

Fortunately, God has blessed me with so many wonderful holidays since, that it's a wonder I remember the "frightful four" at all!

Chapter Eleven

Just Hanging Out

When Lewis and I were growing up, Mom and Dad told us many times to be careful with whom we hung out. They used the old adages: "*You're known by the company you keep; remember who you are*; and *if you don't want to slip, don't go into slippery places.*" And my personal favorite: "*Don't hang out in places you wouldn't want to take Jesus or hang out with people you wouldn't want Him to meet.*"

Years before the popularity of the phrase WWJD (What Would Jesus Do?) came about, before those letters were inscribed onto bracelets, before the four letters became a byword of an entire generation, Mom and Dad would ask Lewis and me that question any time they did not necessarily approve of what we had been doing or were about to do. We were asked to consider the consequences of what our actions would do to our reputation. Would God be pleased or disappointed, or how would we feel afterward?

One of these situations came up when I was about ten or eleven years old. I came up with something that I thought would be funny to do at the time. I did not consider the consequences, nor did I think about whether Jesus would have done something similar when He was my age. When He was twelve years old, He was found by his mother Mary and his step-father Joseph talking with the teachers in the temple and actually teaching them.

It was summertime and we were out of school. Lewis was raking hay for our Uncle Rex, Dad was at work, and I was home with no playmate. I went into the house through the kitchen and saw my mother standing in front of the kitchen sink washing dishes. The window at the sink overlooked the backyard at a tall locust tree that stood in the fence row by the granary.

I stood there a few moments observing her work and a plan popped into my head. I said, "Mom, I feel kind of tired. I think I'll go into my room and lie down for awhile."

"What's the matter, Honey?" Mom asked in her customary concern. She came over to me and like all mothers do, placed the palm of her hand on my forehead to check for a fever. "You don't feel hot!"

"Oh, I'm not hot or anything," I responded. "I just feel sort of yucky. It might be the heat. I think if I lie down for awhile I'll be okay."

"Alright," she said. "I'll check on you later."

I left the kitchen and looked back around the corner of the door to make sure she returned to her work. Once I was sure that she had become absorbed again in what she was doing, I went to my room and closed the door. I removed the clothes I was wearing and dressed in others. After putting a couple of pillows underneath the covers to look like a body was there, I raised the window beside my bed and went through it. I slid down onto a milking stool that I had previously placed underneath the window in case there was some mischief that crossed my mind. I ran around the house with the clothes that I had taken off in my hands. Staying close to the house I went underneath the window where my mother stood washing dishes. I made my way around to the back of the shed where some overflow hay was stored. There I created a life-sized effigy of myself by stuffing the clothes that I had been wearing with straw and dead tree limbs. I crept into the "white building" workshop and grabbed one of the many ropes that hung there on a spike nail that had been driven into one of the two by four studs.

I watched until Mom left the window to gather up more things to clean. Running around to the front of the tractor shed, I climbed the white board fence that surrounded the yard, and hung my effigy by the neck from a limb that stuck straight out from the locust tree. I jumped down from the fence and left the scene just in time. Sneaking into the screened-in porch that ran the full length of that wing of the house where the kitchen was, I came up to the glass storm door and watched to see what reaction my "hanging" scene was going to have.

What I got was not exactly what I wanted. A scream maybe or even a yell would have sufficed, but what I got was worse. When Mom looked out the window toward the locust tree and saw the figure hanging from the tree limb, she fell straight backward and hit the floor like a tree being felled.

Straight out, she went unconscious. I know now that when the eyes see something the mind cannot handle, the mind shuts down.

Hoping and praying that she would come around soon, I had to hurry! I ran through the screen door of the porch to the back yard, climbed the wooden plank fence, and untied the rope that was holding the straw stuffed effigy. With my straw figure in my grasp I jumped to the ground and ran around to the back of the tractor shed. There I removed the tree limbs and straw from the effigy and shook the cloths to remove any remnants of my misdeed. Not to be seen, I ran the long way around the house to the window to my room.

Planning ahead, I had left the window unlocked and slightly ajar. I raised the window and climbed back into my room. After pulling the window down and securing the lock, I removed the clothes I had on and redressed in the clothes used to make the effigy. I threw the clothes I had been wearing onto the floor of the closet, pulled the pillows from underneath the covers, jumped back into bed, and pulled the covers up to my nose and closed my eyes.

It was none too soon. A moment after I had pulled the covers up and taken a deep breath my mother came into my room. She came over to the bed and stood over me for what seemed an eternity. Finally, she bent down and kissed me on the forehead, tiptoed across the floor to the door, and pulled it shut behind her.

I let out a sigh of relief and stayed in my room for well over an hour. When I could not stand to stay in there any longer, I came out. My mom was sitting in a Boston rocker in the den crocheting a green and yellow afghan. She looked at me and asked with those warm mother eyes, "Are you feeling better?"

Feeling guilty as sin, I answered, "Yes, Mom. I feel fine now. I think I'll go outside for awhile."

"Don't go off too far," she said lovingly, "it will soon be milking time."

"In that case," I said, now feeling sick at my stomach from my guilt. "I think I'll go ahead and bring the cows into the barn."

I went through the kitchen and out the same door from wince I had witnessed Mom hit the floor when she had fainted.

After I had finished my chores and Dad and Lewis had come home, we all sat down for dinner. Halfway through the meal, Mom said to Dad, "I had the strangest experience today."

"Yeah, what kind of experience?" he asked, not interrupting the rhythm of shoveling dinner into his mouth.

"I was standing in front of the kitchen window washing dishes," she began as she relived the incident. "I looked up and saw Larry hanging from a limb in that locust tree beside of the tractor shed. He was hanging there with a rope around his neck."

Dropping his fork onto his plate, Dad asked, "You saw what?"

My brother echoed the question, and both asked, "How could that be? Larry's sitting at the table with us."

"I know," Mom answered. She shook her head and stared off into space for a moment and then said, "When I saw what I thought was Larry hanging there, I keeled over backwards. I went out like a light."

"Did you hurt yourself, Mom?" Lewis asked with that concern only he could concoct to gain her favor.

"Mostly my pride was hurt. My rear end and the back of my head are a little sore from hitting the floor," she answered with a chuckle. "When I came to, I got up and went back to the window. There was no Larry or anything else hanging in that tree. I rushed to his room and found him fast asleep in his bed."

"Wow! That's spooky," Lewis commented.

"What do you think happened, Violet?" Dad asked with real concern. "Where you hallucinating? Did you eat something that might have caused you to see something that wasn't there? Were you daydreaming and envisioning something that seemed real?"

"I honestly don't know," she replied. "I do know one thing…."

I had just filled my mouth with some beans, milk and cornbread when she said, "I do know one thing." My stomach knotted up. I coughed and blew the entire contents in my mouth halfway across the table. I thought I was going to swallow my tongue. I was sick to think that she might have figured out the trick that I had played on her. My mouth became so dry that I could hardly swallow. Tears started flowing from my eyes like water cascading over a dam. I continued with a jag of coughing. My brother, who was sitting beside me, began hitting me on my back with the palm of his hand.

"Are you alright, Larry?" Mom asked. "You are as pale as a ghost!"

"Yeah! I'm alright," I spluttered. I turned to Lewis and said, "You can stop hitting me on the back now. I'm alright. I was just listening and not paying attention to my chewing. Some milk ran down the back of my throat and I got choked, that's all."

"After I saw what I thought I saw today," Mom said, "I don't need you choking and dying on me, you hear me?" She then started to cry.

Talking about feeling lower than a snake's belly, I felt worse than you can even imagine! I not only had caused my mother to pass out cold, but worse still, I had caused her to cry. 'What kind of monster am I anyway,' I thought. 'Who would do something so dastardly that it would make their mother faint away and make them cry?'

I glanced at Lewis and he was looking at me with that all-knowing look. I don't know how, but he knew. He knew that Mom had not seen a vision, or had imagined me hanging from a limb of the locust tree in the back yard. He knew that somehow I had done something to make Mom see what she had seen, and it wasn't a mirage or an illusion.

'Oh sickness of sicknesses! What am I going to do? If Lewis has figured this whole thing out, he will not just let it go. He will make certain that both Mom and Dad understand just what a monster I really am and what a saint he is. Oh God,' I thought, 'this is it. He will finally get what he has always wanted – me castigated and humiliated and made to live in the basement.'

"Where were you, Larry, when Mom saw her vision?" Lewis asked.

'Oh, here it comes!' I thought. 'Why are you doing this? I felt that he was already Mom and Dad's favorite. You can do anything,

229

fix anything, and make anything. Why bring me down? I'll be your slave! Please, oh please, don't rat me out!'

I squeaked out, "I wasn't feeling well. I was in bed taking a nap."

"Man," he said as if in deep thought, "Mom knew exactly where you were and still she had such a weird vision! That's incredible."

"Isn't it though," I said staring into my plate. "Maybe the heat got to her as well. I am pretty sure that was why I wasn't feeling so well."

"Yeah, the heat of the day," he mused. "Must have been the heat of the day."

We finished our meal. I helped Mom with the dishes. As a family we watched *Gunsmoke* and *Lawrence Welk.* It was then time for bed.

Lewis and I shared a bedroom. Our beds were bunk beds, his on the top and mine on the bottom. After we had been in bed for a half hour or so, Lewis asked me, "What do you think happened to Mom today?"

Feeling my guilt, I blabbered way too much, "How should I know? Why would you ask me that question? I was in bed taking a nap. Who knows why mothers see what they see or think what they think? Am I a psychic? Do you think that I should know everything?"

"Okay, okay," my brother interjected. "I was just wondering about what happened that's all. Why are you acting so guilty, anyway?"

"Because you know, that's why," I answered and instantly slapped my hand over my mouth.

"Of course I know," Lewis said laughing. "You should have gotten all the straw off the floor if you didn't want someone to figure out that what Mom saw was a stuffed figure of you."

"Oh my God," I cried. "Please Lewis, don't tell Mom! I am so ashamed!"

"Why?" Lewis asked. "I think it's funny. You must have done some serious moving to pull this off. How did you do it anyway?"

I related the whole sordid story to him of how I had made sure that Mom had seen what I was wearing before I had gone to my room, how I had changed clothes and sneaked out the window, how I had stuffed my clothes with straw and broken tree limbs to make a figure that resembled a person, how I had hung my effigy by a rope onto the tree limb, how I had watched Mom faint away, and how in a panic I had reversed everything with lightening speed.

"I can tell you one thing, Lewis," I said matter-of-factly, "I'll never do anything like that again. When Mom keeled over, I almost fainted myself. She scared me half to death. After I had climbed back through the window into our room and got back into bed, I cannot tell you how relieved I was when she came in to check on me. I pretended to be asleep. When she leaned over and kissed me on the forehead, I thought that I would burst into tears. She was showing me such love after I had almost given her a heart attack."

"Don't beat yourself up too much, Larry," my big brother advised. "After all, neither Mom nor Dad know that it was us shooting bee bees at the scrotum on that bull that caused him to stop taking any interest in servicing the cows, that it was a cherry bomb that caused 'Ole Mousie to go dry, and any host of other things that we have done separately and together. We learn our lessons and know better next time. We need our mother so I do hope that you won't do what you did today ever again."

"Oh, you can count on that," I said ashamedly. "I guess it was one of those times when if I had asked the question, 'Would Jesus ever do such a thing?' I would never have done it."

Chapter Twelve

Memories

After telling you the adventures that Lewis and I had with Mom and Dad when using dynamite and how we had reduced a ferocious bull to a pussycat, I feel spent. Mom and Dad have passed. Sharing the crazy stories about the things we used to do with them, especially Dad, floods my soul with so many precious memories.

Oh how I miss seeing them. Holidays and even regular days are just not the same now. I can't send my mom Mother's Day cards or Dad, Father's Day cards anymore. I can't randomly pick up the phone to call and say that I love them any longer. I can't gift Dad with the satin-lined fleece shirts he liked so much. I can't tell Mom that I had just gotten there three or four times in one afternoon. Nothing will ever be the same.

I feel that I cannot burden my wife with these feelings. A mere six weeks before my mother died from the complications of Alzheimer's, my wife's brother, Tommy, who was ten years her junior, killed himself.

There was much speculation. He left no note. He had simply taken his shotgun and the Bible that my wife had given to him many years before, the one filled with cards and pictures that she had sent to him, and had parked his car in a church parking lot, a church he did not even attend. There, early in the morning hours of July 1, 2005, he ended his life.

His soul must have been tremendously tormented to have succumbed to such a desperate act. Regardless of his reasons, those who are left behind to ponder the whys and wherefores are hurt more than those of us who have lost a loved one to a natural cause.

The death of our parents probably hit my brother the hardest. He was the one who was there for them every single day for their last few years of life. He was the one who had taken them everywhere, to visit one or more doctors every week, to hire the caregivers, and to make sure they were fulfilling their duties. Lewis and his sweet wife, Betty, had to pay Mom and Dad's bills, balance their checkbook, monitor their banking, and on and on ad infinitum.

During the same period, Betty's mother was suffering from "old age" and cancer. My brother and his wife had to be there for her as much as they were for Mom and Dad. Betty's mother died first and they had to make all the arrangements for her funeral and burial. The events they had to deal with daily seemed more than any couple should have to handle, but handle it they did.

To watch his wife's mother and his own mother waste away is a lot for anyone to deal with. At least it helps ease the pain when you know in your heart they have gone on to be with the Lord.

On the other hand, suicide is never welcome. Those left behind are devastated and feel robbed of even being able to say goodbye. It feels like they didn't matter enough to have kept them alive or that their love somehow was not enough. As I write this, it has been over four and a half years since Tommy's suicide. My wife and her family still struggle with it almost every day.

One must never lose sight of how miserable or how alone that person must have felt. They might have despised or loathed themselves for something they may have done that caused them to feel unforgivable. Right or wrong, they may have felt that they had disappointed God so much that even though He could forgive them, they could not forgive themselves.

It's our pride and selfishness that causes us to do such heinous things. This of course is how Satan fell and how the first man, Adam, fell - pride and selfishness. At that moment when our sins overwhelm us, we don't consider the people who love us and would do anything to help. Our pride tells us that we have to be in control and put an end to our suffering; our selfishness leads us to forget our loved ones who are robbed of their chance to help us or the opportunity to say goodbye. Our prayer is that Tommy is with Jesus, waiting to welcome us to Heaven with open arms.

* * * * * *

It seems like a lifetime has passed since those crazy days when Lewis and I roamed the hills in Carroll County, Virginia, playing cowboys and Indians, cops and robbers, soldier combatants, safari adventurers, or explorers. Decades have slipped away since we shot copperheads from the hip, bagged groundhogs that were grazing near their dens, plucked grey squirrels from hickory trees with solitary buckshot, caught mountain trout with our bare hands, or dinged rabbits running zig zag from brush piles. Yes, it's been a long time since we operated tractors over land considered by most too steep on which to work, hauled tons of rock off the land to make it ready for planting, turned violent bovines into docile creatures, or used dynamite the way most people used a pickaxe.

There is no doubt that like the sparrow, God always kept His eye upon us. Indeed, His Spirit guided and protected us all our lives. No matter how foolishly we behaved, no matter how dangerous the situation, no matter how far out on a limb we would go, there was always a net to catch us. A supernatural feeling prevented us from making the next step that would have led to disaster; a miraculous intercession shut the mouths of poisonous snakes when we were eye to eye and nose to nose; a superhuman strength helped one of us pull the other out of a dire situation; and a divine intervention kept us safe for such a time as this.

Everything was possible, not only by the supernatural guidance and protection of Almighty God, but also because of the care and instruction of parents who loved their children enough to give them their lead. They gave us a temporal knowledge of Jesus Christ; they obeyed the command of Scripture not to spare the rod which would spoil the child; they set the moral example and the Christian model for us to follow into adult life; and finally, they lived their lives in such a way that when the end came, an entire town had nothing but respect and admiration for them. How true the learned adage, "If a man has a reputation that is not good, he has nothing at all."

When my brother, sister, and I get together now, since the passing of Mom and Dad, we sit around recalling the sweet, sweet memories. They provide us with a celebration of life lived graciously, a commemoration of over seven decades of marital commitment, a giving of esteem and honor, a Mardi gras of lives lived for the King, and a closure to the regrets for childhood pranks.

To know without any doubt that your parents did the best they could, sacrificed so that your life would be better, and never wavered from the path that God had set for them to follow is precious indeed. Knowing they both are walking and talking daily with our Lord and Savior Jesus Christ gives peace to the mind and solace to the soul. We all feel blessed by having that knowledge.

Thank you Mom and thank you Dad for giving us your best. Thank you for your unselfish sacrifices, for the training in the things of God, for instilling in us a good work ethic, and a moral and visual acuity of the fact that God loves us. Because of you we have tried to walk circumspectly and run the race that has been set before us, looking always for the prize of the upward call, to possess and intimately know the Lord Jesus Christ.

One cannot write a book fast enough it seems before events occur that change the ending. Recently Lewis and I conducted the funeral for our sister's husband, Elmo. Mo's health had deteriorated greatly over the last two years. His kidneys were "blown out" by years of taking medication for hypertension. He had been receiving dialysis treatments three days a week for several years. With vein after vein collapsing and portal after portal becoming infected, two weeks prior to his death the dialysis was discontinued.

Fortunately this family knows that to be absent from the body is to be present with the Lord. To continue placing needles into an already racked body that cries out in pain every time the procedure is begun is cruel and is laced with selfishness.

Elmo died surrounded by his family who loved him so very much; they chose to let him go and pass into the presence of the Lord.

Before the funeral actually started, neither my brother nor I had a clear vision of what we should say. Lewis and I had participated in both Mom and Dad's funerals, and God had clearly given us what we should and needed to say hours before their funerals. This time, however, we spent a sleepless night before the funeral service praying and wondering what we would say. It wasn't until each of us got up at the funeral to speak that what we were to say became clear. Perhaps it was more difficult this time because Lewis and I grew up with Elmo. He had always been around; he had always been in the family. It was if he were our big brother. I was three and Lewis was six when Elmo married our sister.

Standing behind the podium above the beautiful walnut coffin that contained the remains of my brother-in-law, I looked down at my sister sitting there on the front pew. She was dressed all in black and tears were just about to flow over the rim of her eyes. A look of pain was on her face. I had no desire to speak the "customary" words of comfort expected from the preacher. Instead, I wanted to rush down from the pulpit and smother my sister with hugs and kisses, to absorb all her pain, and melt away her sorrow and grief. I wanted my brother to join in so the three of us could block out the world that was closing in upon us. I wanted God's promises of no more pain, no more tears, no more sorrows right there and then, without having to go home to be with the Lord. That peace and that comfort are the things I desire someday for all God's children. At that moment in time, however, seeing the burden of grief smothering my sister like a covering of makeup made me want desperately to quickly remove it once and for all.

Then my eyes looked beyond my sister and I gazed for a moment into the eyes of my wife sitting behind her. The tightness in my chest increased and the lump in my throat expanded so that I could hardly breathe. My mind raced out of control and I thought, 'How can my sister just sit there with such composure? Why doesn't she swoon? What if something happened to Charlotte? If my spouse died, my heart would explode! I would want to join her in Heaven right then.'

All talking had ceased in that sanctuary and every eye had become focused on me. No one even coughed. I was completely unsettled by the anticipation. Everyone's breathing became deeper and louder. Air moved in and out of their lungs like the sound created in your own head when breathing oxygen through the hose of a scuba tank under water. The faces of the people attending the funeral began to take on odd shapes as if their skin was being pulled and stretched in all different directions. The walls of the room resembled the sides of a great bellows heaving in and out. The distance from the pulpit to the rear of the chapel became greater and greater until I could hardly make out the faces of those on the last row of seats. I leaned forward on the podium to steady myself. My stomach turned a flip and then uprighted. Ultimately everything returned to normal and calmness settled on me like a fog settles over a moor before dawn. Out of the perfect stillness God whispered to me, "Read my Word."

"We know that if our earthly body were destroyed, we have a body given to us by God, a body not made with hands. It is eternal in the heavens...for we walk by faith, not by sight, and we are confident, that to be absent from the body is to be present with the Lord. (2 Corinthians 5:6-8)"

During a service that lasted forty-five minutes, three songs were sung, and Lewis and I spoke words of comfort to a wife who had lost her husband, to two adult children who had lost their father, to a woman and a man who had lost their brother, and to precious grandchildren whose "Papa" was now gone. The words we spoke were given to us by God and as we spoke them, we too were comforted.

At the funeral home and at the reception in my sister's home, faces that had been unfamiliar at Mom's funeral four years ago, more familiar at Dad's funeral three years ago, now were faces of people I knew, and we all shared something in common. We were either relatives or dear friends of these lives that had come to an end on earth.

Life is short, oh too short. We can write about those times of our youth when the world was our oyster and our lives were invincible, but none of that rings true or holds water. Like the Teacher says to us in Ecclesiastes, *"Vanity of vanities...all is vanity. What profit has a man from all his labor which he takes under the sun? One generation passes away and another generation begins, but the earth abides forever."*

Vanity is the key word here. It means different things to different people. To some it may mean futility, and to others, meaninglessness, or emptiness, or nothingness, or absurdity. As King Solomon gives us his observation of life, he exhibits little profit and accomplishment. When he says **all** is vanity, it must not be taken to mean everything in the universe is vanity because his observations are clearly limited to what he had observed, what he had heard, and what he had lived.

The one verse in Ecclesiastes that says it all is verse 2a of Chapter Three, *"To everything there is a season, and a time to every purpose under heaven: a time to be born and a time to die."*

Solomon reflects on all of life and expresses fourteen antithetical pairs of events behind which God has a sovereign design. When it is one's time to die, if they are a child of God, as Elmo was, then dying is not a problem. *"To be absent from the body **is** to be present with the Lord."*

Our entire family (thank you, Lord) has responded to Jesus the Christ when the call came to their hearts. Because of that, death has lost its sting. What we have after a loved one has gone on to be with the Lord is not regret or fear or wonder. What we have is joy and fond memories, precious memories. Unseen angels send us memories that comfort us, and they linger ever near us so that the sacred past unfolds. Our precious fathers, our loving mothers, and every family member with whom we have shared something during the short time we have traveled here on earth flies across the years and reminds us of old home scenes and of our childhood. That's when the fond memories appear.

As I have traveled on the pathway of life, I have never known what the years may hold. One thing I have come to know, however, is that as I ponder over these things, hope grows fonder and precious memories rush over me like water rushing over the rocks in a stream. Solomon may have thought life is all vanity, but I do not. The things we learn along the way, the friends we make, the closeness of family members, the adventures made with a brother, can never be taken away. It all produces memories, and memories are never brought to mind in vain.

"May the LORD bless you, and keep you, the LORD make His face shine upon you, and be gracious unto you; the LORD lift up His countenance upon you, and give you peace (Numbers 6:24-26)."

About the Author

Dr Vass, a graduate of Virginia Tech in Blacksburg, Virginia and of the Medical College of Virginia School of Dentistry in Richmond, Virginia, has been a practicing dentist since 1973. A year after graduating dental school, Dr. Vass completed an internship in Oral Surgery and Anesthesiology at Saint Agnes Hospital in Baltimore, Maryland. After extensive study of the malady Temporomandibular Joint Pain Dysfunction Syndrome, Dr. Vass wrote the book Temporomandibular Joint Pain Dysfunction Syndrome: Its Diagnosis and Treatment, printed in 1985. Before that book, his article Facial Pain: A Misdiagnosis, was published in the Journal of General Dentistry, 1976.

His latest book, A Reformed View of the Sovereignty of God in a Postmodern World was published and released in February, 2008. It is available online at Amazon.com, Barnes & Nobel.com, PublishAmerica.com, etc.

Dr. Vass grew up in the church, the son of a Primitive Baptist preacher. After finishing his seminary work at Trinity Theological Seminary in Newburgh, Indiana, Dr. Vass graduated from the University of Liverpool, England in 2001 with a Masters of Divinity. He immediately started work toward his PhD in Religious Studies. It was while writing many research papers that Dr. Vass realized that he had a passion for writing and had received a calling to write books pertaining to spiritual matters.

Dr. Vass has been the pastor of Grace Chapel at Southwinds, White Plains, Maryland for four years. He and his wife, Charlotte, a retired executive with the country's largest mall developer, have three children and two grandchildren.

A skier, a scuba diver, and a traveler, but Dr. Vass' greatest love (besides his wife, children, and grandchildren) is writing and doing the research for his books.

Dr. Vass and his wife live in LaPlata, Maryland, a bedroom community of Washington, D.C.